Low-Fat
Dips & Spreads

THE LOW-FAT KITCHEN

LOW-FAT
DIPS & SPREADS

Over 70 Healthy and Delicious Recipes
for Dunking and Slathering

JODY WEATHERSTONE

Clarkson Potter/Publishers
New York

For the Hee-Her

Thanks to my editor, Katie Workman, and everyone at Clarkson Potter who worked on this book. Thanks to Charles Pierce for introducing me to Katie! Special thanks to my good friends Amy Lord and Bruce Weinstein for their suggestions and advice. And as always, thanks to my beloved husband, James, for his enduring support and good taste.

Published by Clarkson N. Potter/Publishers, 201 East 50th Street, New York, New York 10022. Member of the Crown Publishing Group.

Random House, Inc. New York, Toronto, London, Sydney, Auckland

CLARKSON N. POTTER, POTTER, and colophon are trademarks of Clarkson N. Potter, Inc.

Printed in the U.S.A.

Design by Susan DeStaebler

Library of Congress Cataloging-in Publication Data is available upon request.

ISBN 0-517-70485-4

10 9 8 7 6 5 4 3 2 1

First Edition

Contents

Introduction

Our notion of what a dip is has come a long way from the days of sour cream blended with onion soup mix accompanied by nacho-flavored chips and celery sticks. We now know that a low-fat diet is a necessary way to eat for a healthy, happy life, and this understanding has impacted strongly on what we want to eat, whether at a family meal, a party, or a restaurant. Also, the influence of different cultures on American tastes has inspired a desire to try new flavors and ways of eating, and just about every culture has some variety of dip or spread, whether it be a salsa, chutney, tapenade, or fondue.

Dips and spreads are perfect party foods since most can be made ahead of time. They are usually based on inexpensive ingredients, and they can also stretch an expensive ingredient, such as smoked salmon, a long way. Some are very light and and refreshing while others are much more substantial, making for a varied buffet. Many are made in a few easy steps, often in one bowl, and a large number do not require cooking, making them perfect for hot-weather entertaining.

And beyond cocktail parties, dips and spreads can be the basis of a relaxed picnic or a light meal. There is an endless number of ways to pair them with all sorts of dippers and "spreadees," for lack of a better term. Many also make great sandwiches, alone or combined with different cheeses, meats, or grilled vegetables. Others are perfect accompaniments to grilled meats and fish or are excellent burger toppings.

However, dips and spreads are traditionally laden with fat, being based on cheeses, sour cream, mayonnaise, and olive oil. Fortunately, this does not have to be the case. There are many excellent reduced-fat products available today that can be substituted for the original. Also, lots of dips do not rely on fat for their flavor or texture, instead using ingredients like pureed vegetables or small amounts of very flavorful oils to make them delicious and satisfying. This book contains lightened versions of familiar favorites, as well as dips and spreads that are inspired by other cultures or interpretations of other dishes.

Many recipes call for low-fat or nonfat dairy products such as sour cream, mayonnaise, cream cheese, ricotta cheese, cottage cheese, and Cheddar and mozzarella. Sometimes I call for low-fat and sometimes nonfat. In some cases this is because one may give a better result in the recipe, and in others, it is in order to keep the fat content under 30 percent. Low-fat hard cheeses, such as Cheddar and mozzarella, are always a better choice than the nonfat variety, as the nonfat ones do not melt properly or have an appealing texture. Nonfat cottage cheese and yogurt are excellent, however, and nonfat yogurt works perfectly for making yogurt cheese (page 40).

Different brands vary very slightly in their fat and calorie contents, so the analysis given should be read as an average. However, all of the brands are fairly comparable in terms of nutritional content, so the analysis will not be too different no matter which kind you choose. Taste a variety of brands until you find the ones you like best.

The nutritional analysis given with each recipe is for a serving size of 2 tablespoons. If a choice of ingredients is given, such as low-fat *or* nonfat cottage cheese, the analysis is based on the first listing. All optional ingredients have been included in the nutritional breakdown as well.

And remember, there are no rules. Use these recipes as starting places to create your own delicious dips and spreads. Experiment and enjoy the unlimited possibilities!

DIP AND SPREAD BASICS

Food processor. Many of the recipes here call for the use of a food processor. A blender can be substituted, with slightly different results, but be sure to chop ingredients into small pieces before adding them and work in batches if necessary, mixing the blended batches by hand at the end.

How much to make. A good rule of thumb when serving appetizers at a cocktail party is to make three to four dishes for parties of fifteen to eighteen, adding another dish for every five people after that. Allow about ten "bites" per person if you are not serving a meal afterward. All of the recipes here can be easily doubled.

Nonstick spray. The olive oil variety is excellent, imparting a light flavor without the fat, and the vegetable oil version has a very mild, unobtrusive flavor. Avoid the butter-flavored type, as it is not suited to any of the recipes here. Use the sprays lightly.

Preparing ahead. Most of the recipes in this book can be made in advance. In fact, many need time to chill, and actually improve with a day to let the flavors meld. If a recipe says to serve at room temperature, be sure to allow about thirty minutes for it to return to room temperature after removing it from the refrigerator.

INGREDIENT INFORMATION

Avocado. Hass (California) avocados are smallish with bumpy green skin that blackens as they ripen. I prefer their sweet, buttery flesh to Fuerte (Florida) avocados, which are large, green, and smooth, with a higher water content, although either will suffice.

Citrus zest. When zesting citrus fruits, use only the thin colored skin and not the bitter white "pith" that lies just underneath. Use a zester, a fine grater, a paring knife, or a vegetable peeler to remove the zest, which can then be sliced thin or minced as needed.

Garlic. Regular white garlic and purple garlic are quite strong, while elephant garlic is somewhat milder. The flavor of raw garlic becomes stronger with age, so if you are making a dip ahead of time, you might want to lessen the amount slightly and then adjust the amount when you are ready to serve it.

Spices. Spices retain the most flavor when stored whole. I use a coffee grinder reserved just for this purpose to grind spices as I need them. The flavor is also intensified by lightly toasting the whole seeds in a dry skillet until fragrant just before grinding. Remember that cold food needs more seasoning than hot, as heat activates the seasonings, so be sure to taste the dips and spreads after chilling and adjust the seasonings if necessary.

Stock or broth. All of the recipes here were tested using reduced-sodium defatted chicken or beef stock. There are some good canned varieties available, or, if you make your own, you can easily degrease it. Once your homemade stock has cooled to room temperature, refrigerate it until the fat hardens and can be lifted off. The fat can also be removed by ladling off the top layer while the stock is cooling or by laying paper towels on top to soak up the grease. Stock can be stored in the freezer for up to six months, or kept refrigerated for several days.

Tofu. Tofu, or soybean curd, is sold packaged or fresh usually in ten-ounce blocks. Store fresh tofu immersed in cold water in the refrigerator. Change the water every day and it will keep for up to ten days. Tofu also comes in different densities, ranging from soft to firm. For the recipes in this book, you will need the soft variety. Now low-fat tofu is available and should be used where specified.

Salt. I have left the amount of salt up to the cook in most cases, as I find people's tastes vary greatly in this area. I prefer to use kosher salt, which has larger granules and a purer flavor than regular table salt, making the amount easier to control.

Menu Suggestions

I love to serve dips in natural vegetable and bread "bowls" made by hollowing out various vegetables, fruits, and large rustic loaves of bread. Not only does it make a beautiful presentation, but it saves time washing dishes! Vegetables suitable for this include these:

*Red, green, yellow, and purple bell peppers • Eggplants
Purple and white cabbage • Small pumpkins
Acorn and butternut squash • Cantaloupe and honeydew melons*

A simple and plentiful way of presenting an assortment of dips is to accompany them with lots of dippers. I like to put out three large baskets. One overflows with small slices of all sorts of breads: rye, pumpernickel, French, raisin, whole grain, pita, and marble. Another is a basket of crudités: carrots; radishes; steamed asparagus, broccoli, and cauliflower; button mushrooms; red bell peppers; jicama; and sugar snap peas. A third basket contains all sorts of crackers and flatbreads. Your guests can decide what they want to dip or spread with what. And definitely look at the dipper recipes in the last chapter. Most require a bit of cooking or preparation time, but they can help turn dips and spreads into more substantial hors d'oeuvres fare, even a light meal.

A Colorful Dip Buffet
*Ruby Beet Terrine • Broccoli and Tarragon Dip
Taramasalata • Provençal Saffron-Scented Dip*

A Champagne Toast
*Salmon Mousse • Three-Vegetable Terrine
Roasted Red Pepper Mousse • Assorted Crostini*

Asian Theme
*Asian Butternut Squash Puree • Chinese Green Bean and
Garbanzo Spread • Sesame-Tofu Dip • Sirloin Satay*

Brunch

Smoked Trout Pâté • Honey-Vanilla Yogurt Spread
Burgundy-Pear Butter • Light Wheat Scones

Picnic on a Hot Summer Day

(Turkey Burgers with) Papaya and Cilantro Salsa
Plum Tomato and Mint Salsa • Roasted Red Pepper Catsup
Pretzels and Bagel Chips

Mexican

Chunky Black Bean Dip • Tequila Pico de Gallo
Green Pea Guacamole • Curly Baked Tortillas

Greek

Hummus • Taramasalata • Tzatziki
Warm Whole Wheat and White Pita Bread

Provençal

Brandade de Morue • Anchoiade
Provençal Saffron-Scented Dip • Baguettes

Italian

Basil Pesto Spread • Roasted Garlic Puree
Eggplant Caviar • Garlic-Rubbed Crostini

Great Sandwiches

Herbed Turkey Pâté on Rye
Hummus in a Pita with Sprouts and Tomato
Smoked Trout Pâté on an Onion Bagel

Dips as Pasta Sauces

Basil Pesto Spread • Sun-Dried Tomato Spread
Roasted Tomato and Olive Spread

Vegetable Dips
and Spreads

Eggplant Caviar

*R*oasting the eggplant along with the garlic and rosemary not only intensifies the flavor but simplifies the cooking as well. Feel free to add other herbs to the pan. This is a great place to use up stems from bunches of parsley and basil.

Try serving this dip in endive leaves or on bread rounds topped with thinly sliced cucumber.

1 large eggplant (about 2 pounds), cut in half lengthwise	*1 large sprig of fresh rosemary*
Salt and black pepper	*16 sun-dried tomatoes (dry, not packed in oil)*
1 whole head of garlic, unpeeled	*2 tablespoons lemon juice*
	1/2 teaspoon dried oregano

Preheat the oven to 400°F. and lightly coat a baking pan with nonstick cooking spray. Sprinkle the eggplant with salt and pepper and place, cut side down, in the pan. Spray the garlic lightly with the oil, sprinkle with salt and pepper, and place in the pan along with the rosemary. Cover with foil and bake for 1 hour, until the garlic and eggplant are very tender. Uncover and allow to cool at room temperature.

Place the sun-dried tomatoes in a small bowl and pour in just enough boiling water to cover. Let stand 5 minutes. Drain, reserving the liquid, and coarsely chop the tomatoes.

When the eggplant is cool enough to handle, scrape out the pulp and place in a food processor. Cut off the top of the garlic using a serrated knife and squeeze out the pulp. Add to the food processor along with the sun-dried tomatoes, lemon juice, oregano, 1 teaspoon salt, and 1/2 teaspoon pepper. Process until pureed. Add a small amount of the tomato soaking liquid to reach the desired consistency.

Transfer to a bowl and chill. This dip is best if allowed to chill overnight, as the flavors become stronger and more balanced with time. Season to taste with additional salt, pepper, and lemon juice, if desired.

MAKES 2 ½ CUPS (20 SERVINGS)
Per serving: 34 calories (7% from fat), fat: 0.2g, carbohydrates: 7.07g, protein: 1.32g

Basil Pesto Spread

*E*verybody loves pesto! Here is one without all the oil but with all the punch. Add a little Parmesan cheese if you want to splurge a bit.

> 3 to 4 garlic cloves
> 4 cups loosely packed fresh
>   basil leaves
> 5 tablespoons dry bread
>   crumbs
>
> ¼ cup white wine
> 1 teaspoon walnut or extra-
>   virgin olive oil
> Salt and black pepper

Place the garlic cloves in a food processor and process until finely minced. Add the basil leaves and process until finely ground, scraping down the sides as necessary. Transfer to a bowl and add the bread crumbs 1 tablespoon at a time, incorporating well after each addition. Add the wine gradually and stir in the oil. Season with salt and pepper to taste.

MAKES 1 CUP (8 SERVINGS)
Per serving: 33 calories (24% from fat), fat: 0.8g, carbohydrates: 4.1g, protein: 1.06g

Thai Dipping Sauce

The Thai ingredients called for in this pungent dipping sauce are becoming more readily available. Lemongrass can be found in Asian markets as well as some large produce markets. Look for thick, firm, but not dry stalks with a lemony scent.

Thai chilies are about 1 inch long, either red or green, and very hot. Use care when seeding them, and wear plastic gloves. Thai fish sauce is also available in Asian markets and even in some supermarkets in the Asian ingredients section. It smells quite pungent, but has a distinctive, yet surprisingly understated flavor that is irreplaceable. This is a perfect match for Sirloin or Chicken Satay (page 86) as well as dumplings, wontons, or an assortment of grilled vegetables (page 92).

2 stalks of lemongrass
2 Thai chilies, stemmed and
    seeded
1-inch chunk of peeled fresh
    ginger
1 small tomato, seeded and
    coarsely chopped

1 red bell pepper, seeded and
    diced
1 tablespoon sugar
2 tablespoons tomato paste
2 tablespoons fish sauce
1 tablespoon lime juice

Remove the tough outer husks from the lemongrass. Cut off the base of the stalk and the tough, grassy tops, reserving about 6 inches of the stalk to use. Finely chop the lemongrass. Place the lemongrass and the chilies in a small saucepan and cover with 1 cup cold water. Bring to a boil over high heat, lower the heat, and simmer for 5 minutes. Remove from the heat and let stand for 5 minutes more.

In the bowl of a food processor, combine the ginger, tomato, bell pepper, sugar, and tomato paste. Pulse until finely chopped and well blended. Add the contents of the saucepan and process until smooth.

Transfer to a bowl; stir in the fish sauce and lime juice. Allow to cool to room temperature before serving or serve chilled. This dip may be prepared up to a day ahead.

MAKES 2 CUPS (16 SERVINGS)
Per serving: 14 calories (8% from fat), fat: 0.13g, carbohydrates: 2.67g, protein: 0.75g

Roasted Garlic Puree

Preheat the oven to 400°F. and lightly coat a baking pan with non-stick olive oil spray. Place several whole heads of garlic, peels on, in the pan (6 to 8 heads yield about 1 cup garlic puree). Lightly coat the garlic with the olive oil spray and sprinkle with salt. Bake for 50 to 60 minutes, until the tops are lightly browned and very soft to the touch. They will be very fragrant. Cool at room temperature. When cool enough to handle, slice off the top of each head using a serrated knife.

At this point, you can serve the garlic as is. Allow your guests to squeeze or scoop out the pulp from the cloves and spread it on some nice crusty bread. Add a glass of wine and perhaps some olives, and you have a lovely start to a meal.

Alternatively, you can squeeze all of the pulp out into a bowl, mash lightly with a fork, and reserve for use in any of the following recipes calling for roasted garlic.

If you have extra (go ahead, make extra!), freeze it in ice cube trays and when solid, transfer to a plastic bag and store in the freezer so you have small, handy amounts to use whenever you want. One ice cube equals about $1\frac{1}{2}$ tablespoons.

MAKES 1 CUP PUREE (6 TO 8 HEADS OF GARLIC, 8 SERVINGS)
Per serving: 53 calories (3% from fat), fat: 0.18g, carbohydrates: 11.9g, protein: 2.25g

Green Pea Guacamole

*W*hen this idea was suggested to me, I couldn't believe I had never heard it before! It seems such an obvious solution to the high fat content of traditional avocado guacamole. Also, it retains its bright green color for several days, unlike guacamole made from only avocado, which turns brown within half a day.

Serve the guacamole with bell pepper strips, jicama, and baked tortilla chips (page 84).

1 pound (3 cups) peas, fresh or frozen and defrosted
1/2 small Hass avocado, peeled and diced 1/2 inch
1 1/2 tablespoons lime juice
2 tablespoons chopped fresh cilantro
1/4 cup finely diced red bell pepper
Salt and black pepper
Thinly sliced red onion for garnish
Dash of red pepper flakes

Coarsely mash the peas with a potato masher or pulse them several times in a food processor. Place the mashed peas in a food mill set over a bowl, pass through to puree smoothly and to remove the skins. If you do not have a food mill, you can place the peas in a sieve and press them through with a rubber spatula, discarding the skins.

Add the diced avocado to the peas and blend in, coarsely mashing with a fork. Stir in the lime juice, cilantro, and diced red pepper and season to taste with salt and pepper. Cover and chill for at least 1 hour. Garnish with thinly sliced red onion and a dash of red pepper flakes just before serving.

MAKES 1 1/2 CUPS (12 SERVINGS)
Per serving: 43 calories (24% from fat), fat: 1.22g, carbohydrates: 6.5g, protein: 2.06g

Asian Butternut Squash Puree

*T*his unusual combination is one of my favorites. The creamy, buttery texture of the squash will make you want to eat this dip with a spoon. Serve with slices of pumpernickel or marble bread.

*1 medium butternut squash,
   split in half lengthwise*
1 tablespoon soy sauce
1 tablespoon honey

*1 tablespoon tahini
   (sesame paste)*
Salt

Preheat the oven to 400°F. Lightly cover a baking pan with nonstick cooking spray and place the squash, cut side down, in the pan. Bake in the center of the oven for 45 to 60 minutes, until the squash has released liquid and is tender to the touch. Allow to cool.

When the squash is cool enough to handle, scrape out the pulp, discarding the seeds and skin. You should have about 2 cups of squash. Place the squash in a food processor with the soy sauce, honey, tahini, and salt to taste and process until just smooth. Do not overprocess or it will become gummy.

Transfer to a bowl, cover, and chill for at least 1 hour. This dip can be made a day ahead.

If any liquid separates from the dip while chilling, simply stir it back in before serving.

MAKES 2 CUPS (16 SERVINGS)
Per serving: 27 calories (17% from fat), fat: 0.5g, carbohydrates: 5.6g, protein: 0.71g

Roasted Red Pepper Catsup

Roasted red peppers can be bought ready to use in jars. However, they are vastly inferior to those made at home. If you have a gas range, this is the simplest of kitchen tasks to perform (and they make your house smell great!). Simply place one or two whole clean peppers right on the burner over a high flame and allow them to char all over, turning frequently with a pair of tongs, until the peppers are completely black. Allow to cool to room temperature. Some people like to place the peppers in a paper bag or a bowl covered with plastic wrap to steam off the skins. However, I do not find this to be necessary. When they are cool enough to handle, peel off the charred skin. Don't worry if some of the black stays on; it gives a pleasant smoky flavor. Stem, seed, and devein and your pepper is ready to use.

Try this catsup with your next burger. It is especially good with turkey burgers and is also a great dip for chilled shrimp or Sirloin or Chicken Satay (page 86).

4 roasted red peppers,
  peeled, seeded, and
  deveined
1 small tomato, diced
1 tablespoon prepared
  horseradish
1 garlic clove
1 teaspoon Worcestershire
  sauce

1/2 teaspoon sugar
1/2 tablespoon red wine
  vinegar
Dash of Tabasco sauce
2 tablespoons chopped fresh
  parsley
Salt and black pepper

Combine the roasted peppers, tomato, horseradish, garlic, Worcestershire sauce, sugar, vinegar, and Tabasco sauce in a food processor and process until pureed. Transfer to a bowl, stir in the parsley, and season with salt and pepper to taste. Cover and chill for 1 hour. This will keep for up to 1 week.

MAKES 2 CUPS (16 SERVINGS)
Per serving: 8 calories (6% from fat), fat: 0.06g, carbohydrates: 1.9g, protein: 0.24g

Broccoli and Tarragon Dip

*B*roccoli and tarragon are a classic pairing. Serve this dip with tiny boiled new potatoes.

1 medium head of broccoli (about 1 pound), cut into florets, stalks peeled and sliced 1 inch thick
²/₃ cup low-fat buttermilk

1 heaping teaspoon dried tarragon
¹/₂ teaspoon salt
³/₄ cup low-fat ricotta cheese
White pepper

Bring a large pot of salted water to a boil. Add the broccoli and boil 6 to 8 minutes, until very tender but still bright green. Drain and run under cold water. Coarsely chop several florets (enough to yield ³/₄ cup) and set aside.

Place the rest of the broccoli florets and stems in a food processor and process until finely chopped. Add the buttermilk, tarragon, and salt and process until smooth.

Transfer to a bowl and stir in the ricotta and reserved chopped florets. Season to taste with pepper and additional salt, if necessary. Cover and chill for at least 2 hours. This dip can be prepared up to a day ahead.

MAKES 3 ¹/₂ CUPS (28 SERVINGS)
Per serving: 13 calories (22% from fat), fat: 0.3g, carbohydrates: 1.3g, protein: 1.3g

Mushroom Spread

Sake is a Japanese rice wine with a mild, yet distinctive flavor. Dry vermouth can be substituted with excellent results.

2 (10-ounce) packages button
    mushrooms, wiped clean
    and quartered
3 large shallots, minced
1 tablespoon minced peeled
    fresh ginger
$1/4$ cup sake (rice wine)
1 tablespoon Worcestershire
    sauce

1 tablespoon soy sauce
$1/2$ teaspoon dried thyme
$1/2$ teaspoon salt
Black pepper
2 tablespoons chopped fresh
    parsley

In a food processor, chop the mushrooms very finely, almost like coarse bread crumbs. You will need to do this in 2 or 3 batches.

Lightly coat a large skillet with nonstick cooking spray. Over medium heat, sauté the shallots until slightly softened, 2 to 3 minutes. Add the ginger and cook 1 minute more, until fragrant. Add the mushrooms, sake, Worcestershire sauce, soy sauce, thyme, and salt and stir to combine. Cook, stirring often, for 15 to 20 minutes. The mixture will release a lot of liquid at first and then begin to dry out. It is done when it feels moist but not watery when pressed against the side of the pan with a wooden spoon.

Transfer to a bowl and allow to cool to room temperature. Season to taste with additional salt, if necessary, and pepper and stir in the chopped parsley. Serve at room temperature.

MAKES 2 CUPS (16 SERVINGS)
Per serving: 17 calories (6% from fat), fat: 0.1g, carbohydrates: 2.7g, protein: 0.82g

Spinach and Feta Cheese Dip

Spinach and feta cheese is a classic Greek pairing that can't be beat! This dip is great presented in a hollowed-out round loaf of black bread, served with chunks of the same bread on the side.

1 (10-ounce) package frozen chopped spinach, thawed and squeezed dry
1 cup nonfat plain yogurt
$\frac{1}{2}$ cup crumbled feta cheese
1 garlic clove, chopped

1 teaspoon dried oregano
$\frac{1}{2}$ teaspoon dried thyme
$\frac{1}{4}$ teaspoon black pepper
Pinch of cayenne
Salt

Combine the spinach, yogurt, feta cheese, garlic, oregano, thyme, pepper, and cayenne in a food processor and pulse until well blended but still slightly chunky. Season with salt to taste.

Transfer to a bowl, cover, and chill at least 1 hour. This dip can be prepared up to 1 day ahead.

MAKES 3 CUPS (24 SERVINGS)

Per serving: 15 calories (30% from fat), fat: 0.54g, carbohydrates: 1.4g, protein: 1.26g

Panzanella Dip

This is sort of a cross between a panzanella, or bread salad, and a gazpacho. Use the best, ripest tomatoes you can find and a good-quality, dense white bread. Serve with Grilled Polenta Wedges (page 88) or endive leaves.

8 slices firm thick white bread, crusts removed

2 large ripe tomatoes, coarsely chopped

1 cucumber

1 yellow or red bell pepper, seeded and diced $1/4$ inch

1 medium onion, finely chopped

$1/4$ cup chopped fresh parsley

$1/2$ cup chopped fresh basil

2 tablespoons capers, drained and rinsed

2 tablespoons lemon juice

3 tablespoons balsamic vinegar

$1/2$ teaspoon sugar

1 tablespoon extra-virgin olive oil

Salt and black pepper

Shaved Parmesan cheese for garnish (optional)

Preheat the oven to 300°F. Cut the bread into $1/2$-inch cubes and spread in a single layer on a baking sheet. Bake for 18 to 20 minutes, shaking the pan occasionally, until the bread is completely dry. Remove from the oven and allow to cool slightly.

Place the tomatoes in the bowl of a food processor and pulse several times until a chunky puree is formed. Transfer to a large bowl.

Peel the cucumber and cut in half lengthwise. Using a spoon, scrape out the seeds from the center of each half and discard. Cut the cucumber into $1/4$-inch dice and add it to the tomato.

Add the bell pepper, onion, parsley, basil, and capers to the tomatoes and toss to combine well. Stir in the lemon juice, balsamic vinegar, sugar, and olive oil.

Place the cooled bread in the food processor and pulse until large coarse crumbs of varying sizes are formed. Do not over-process. Add the bread to the tomato mixture and toss well. Season to taste with salt and pepper. Cover and refrigerate for at least 30 minutes. This dip is best served within a few hours. Garnish with Parmesan curls, if desired.

MAKES 5 CUPS (40 SERVINGS)
Per serving: 24 calories (11% from fat), fat: 0.3g, carbohydrates: 4.65g, protein: 0.8g

Roasted Tomato and Olive Spread

*R*oasting the tomatoes slowly brings out their sweetness while keeping their juiciness. This is great served with slices of crusty baguette or tossed with pasta.

18 to 20 large plum tomatoes, cut in half lengthwise	*1/4 cup finely chopped black olives (about 10 to 12 olives)*
1/2 cup chopped fresh basil	*Salt and black pepper*

Preheat the oven to 300°F. Place the tomatoes on a sheet pan, cut side up, and place in the oven. Bake for 2 to 2½ hours, until the tomatoes are shriveled and dry around the edges but still plump and soft when pressed lightly. Cool to room temperature.

Chop the tomatoes until they are the consistency of a chunky sauce. Be careful; they are very juicy and will squirt you! Blend in the basil and olives. Season to taste with salt and pepper.

MAKES 2 CUPS (16 SERVINGS)
Per serving: 19 calories (21% from fat), fat: 0.5g, carbohydrates: 3.8g, protein: 0.7g

Sun-Dried Tomato Spread

The flavor of sun-dried tomatoes is so concentrated that a little of this spread provides a lot of flavor. Try it on small toasted bread rounds rubbed with a cut clove of garlic. It also is great tossed with pasta.

1/4 pound (about 40) sun-dried tomatoes (dry, not packed in oil)

3 anchovy fillets, rinsed and patted dry

1/3 cup loosely packed fresh basil leaves

1/4 cup loosely packed fresh parsley leaves

1 tablespoon capers, drained and rinsed

10 pitted black olives

1 garlic clove

Black pepper to taste

2 tablespoons balsamic vinegar

1/2 tablespoon extra-virgin olive oil

Place the sun-dried tomatoes in a small bowl and pour just enough boiling water over them to cover. Let stand for 20 to 30 minutes. Drain the tomatoes well, reserving the liquid.

Place the tomatoes in the bowl of a food processor and pulse until coarsely chopped. Add the anchovies, basil, parsley, capers, olives, garlic, and pepper and process until a paste is formed, scraping down the sides as necessary. With the motor running, pour in the vinegar and then the olive oil. If the paste is too thick, add some of the tomato soaking liquid a spoonful at a time, until a spreadable paste is formed.

Transfer to a bowl and serve at room temperature. This spread will keep for up to 2 weeks tightly covered in the refrigerator.

MAKES 1 CUP (8 SERVINGS)
Per serving: 65 calories (25% from fat), fat: 1.8g, carbohydrates: 9.7g, protein: 2.68g

Bean Dips and Spreads

Chunky Black Bean Dip

Canadian bacon, which is much lower in fat than sliced slab bacon, adds a meaty, chililike flavor to this dip. For a smoother consistency, you can transfer the whole dip to the food processor at the end of the recipe and puree. Serve with plenty of crisp baked tortilla chips (page 84), and accompany it with Green Pea Guacamole (page 18) and Tequila Pico de Gallo (page 53) for a Mexican feast!

2 (15-ounce) cans black
  beans, rinsed and drained
1/4 cup beef stock
1 cup seeded and diced
  tomatoes
1/3 cup chopped fresh cilantro

1 small onion, finely chopped
1/2 cup finely diced Canadian
  bacon or cooked ham
1/2 teaspoon ground cumin
Salt and black pepper

In a food processor, combine half of the beans with the beef stock and process until smooth. Transfer to a bowl, stir in the tomatoes and cilantro, and set aside.

Spray a skillet with nonstick cooking spray. Add the onion, bacon, and cumin. Sauté over medium heat, stirring often, until the onion is soft, about 5 minutes. Do not brown. Add the remaining half of the beans and cook 2 to 3 minutes, mashing with a wooden spoon until the mixture is chunky but somewhat creamy.

Add the contents of the skillet to the pureed beans and stir to combine. Season to taste with salt and pepper. Serve at room temperature. This dip can be made up to 2 days ahead and stored tightly covered in the refrigerator. Allow it to come to room temperature before serving.

MAKES 3 1/2 CUPS (28 SERVINGS)
Per serving: 27 calories (13% from fat), fat: 0.3g, carbohydrates: 4.2g, protein: 2.04g

Hummus

*H*ummus is delicious with whole wheat or white pita wedges. It also makes a great sandwich with thinly sliced tomatoes, cucumbers, and alfalfa sprouts. Sesame oil is very high in fat but has a very rich taste, so the ¼ teaspoon called for here adds a lot of flavor but hardly any fat or calories per serving.

2 garlic cloves
2 (16-ounce) cans chickpeas, drained and rinsed
¼ cup tahini (sesame paste)
¼ teaspoon sesame oil

Juice of 2 lemons
½ teaspoon crushed red pepper flakes
Salt and black pepper

Place the garlic in the bowl of a food processor and pulse until minced. Add the chickpeas, tahini, sesame oil, lemon juice, and red pepper flakes. Pulse until a thick pulp is formed. With the motor running, add water in a slow stream until the mixture is a smooth, thick, spreadable paste. This will take ⅓ to ⅔ cup water, depending on the brand and moistness of the chickpeas. Season to taste with salt and pepper.

Transfer to a bowl, cover, and chill until serving (see Note).

MAKES 4 CUPS (32 SERVINGS)
Per serving: 45 calories (27% from fat), fat: 1.4g, carbohydrates: 6.8g, protein: 1.75g

Note. The hummus can easily be made up to 2 days ahead. However, the garlic and red pepper will get stronger as it sits. If a strong flavor is not to your liking, try adding half the amount when making the dip and then adding more to taste when ready to serve.

Provençal Saffron-Scented Dip

This is a refined, subtle dip with a wonderfully smooth texture and an enticing aroma. Serve with a selection of fresh vegetables, such as asparagus, cherry tomatoes, and thinly sliced fennel, and salty olives.

1 large all-purpose potato (about ³/₄ pound), peeled and cut into 1-inch chunks	1 (19-ounce) can cannellini beans, rinsed and drained
¹/₂ cup chicken broth	1 teaspoon salt, plus more to taste
¹/₂ cup orange juice	¹/₂ teaspoon dry mustard
Large pinch of saffron (about ¹/₈ teaspoon)	1 teaspoon orange zest
	Black pepper

Place the potato chunks in a large saucepan and cover with cold salted water. Bring to a boil over high heat and boil for about 12 minutes, until very tender. Drain well.

Combine the chicken broth and orange juice in a small saucepan and bring to a boil. Add the saffron and remove from the heat. Let steep for 10 minutes.

Place the beans, potato, 1 teaspoon salt, and mustard in a food processor. Pulse, scraping down the sides as necessary, until just blended but still lumpy. Do not overprocess. With the motor running, add half the saffron-infused liquid. When smooth, transfer to a bowl.

Add enough of the remaining liquid to reach a smooth, creamy dip consistency. This may or may not take all of the liquid. If it does not, strain and add all of the remaining saffron. Add the orange zest and season to taste with salt and pepper. Cover and chill at least 1 hour. This dip can be made up to 2 days ahead.

MAKES 3 CUPS (24 SERVINGS)
Per serving: 26 calories (6% from fat), fat: 0.18g, carbohydrates: 5.2g, protein: 0.92g

Chinese Green Bean and Garbanzo Spread

*T*his unusual spread calls for Chinese five-spice powder, a blend of star anise, cinnamon, fennel, Szechuan peppercorns, and cloves. Some American brands add other spices as well, such as ginger, but this combination is the authentic one.

Try spreading it on mini rice cakes and topping with shredded surimi seafood, available at the fish counter of many supermarkets.

$^1/_2$ pound green beans, trimmed

1 cup canned garbanzo beans, drained and rinsed

1 shallot, quartered

2 hard-boiled egg whites, coarsely chopped

1 tablespoon soy sauce

1 tablespoon chopped fresh parsley

$^1/_4$ teaspoon Chinese five-spice powder

2 tablespoons chopped fresh cilantro

$^1/_4$ teaspoon sesame oil

Salt and black pepper

Bring a pot of salted water to a boil. Add the green beans and boil for 5 minutes, until tender but still bright green. Drain and rinse.

In a food processor, combine the green beans, garbanzo beans, and shallot. Process until a paste is formed. Add the egg whites, soy sauce, parsley, five-spice powder, cilantro, and sesame oil. Process until a smooth spread is formed. Season to taste with salt and pepper. Transfer to a bowl, cover, and chill for at least 1 hour. This dip can be prepared a day ahead and served chilled or at room temperature.

MAKES 2 CUPS (16 SERVINGS)

Per serving: 25 calories (15% from fat), fat: 0.4g, carbohydrates: 4.05g, protein: 1.46g

Lima Bean and Parsnip Puree

*T*he old-fashioned ingredients in this creamy dip have a surprisingly subtle and sophisticated flavor. Parsnips are in the same family as carrots and you should cook them as you would carrots. Look for parsnips that are crisp, firm, and free of cracks. Since nutmeg is such a potent spice, start by adding a small pinch, then taste the puree and add more if necessary. Serve this dip with fresh bread, crisp bagel chips, or crostini.

1 large parsnip (about $^1/_2$ pound), peeled and cut into 1-inch chunks	$^1/_4$ cup water
	1 tablespoon sugar
1 (10-ounce) package frozen lima beans, defrosted	Zest of 1 lemon
	Dash of grated nutmeg
$^1/_2$ medium onion, finely chopped	Salt and white pepper
	5 to 6 tablespoons low-fat milk

Place the parsnip chunks in a large saucepan and cover with cold water. Bring to a boil over high heat. Lower the heat and simmer, covered, for about 10 minutes, until the parsnips are very tender when pierced with a fork.

Place the lima beans in a colander. Drain the parsnips in the same colander, pouring the hot water over the lima beans. Set aside.

Lightly coat a large skillet with nonstick cooking spray. Add the onions, water, and the sugar. Bring to a simmer over medium heat and cook, stirring often, until the onions are translucent and the sugar and water have become thick and syrupy, about 8 minutes. Add the parsnips, lima beans, lemon zest, and nutmeg. Season with salt and pepper and continue to cook, stirring often, until heated through and well blended, 2 to 3 minutes.

Transfer the contents of the skillet to the bowl of a food processor and process until fairly smooth. With the motor running, add the milk in a slow stream until the mixture is smooth and creamy. Season to taste with salt, pepper, and additional nutmeg, if desired.

Transfer to a bowl and serve at room temperature. This is best served within a day of preparing. If refrigerating, be sure to allow the dip to come to room temperature before serving.

MAKES 2 $\frac{1}{2}$ CUPS (20 SERVINGS)

Per serving: 29 calories (4% from fat), fat: 0.13g, carbohydrates: 6.05g, protein: 1.26g

Moroccan White Bean Dip

Delicious, rich-tasting, and complex, this dip has a similar color and texture to hummus but a completely different combination of flavors that will surprise and delight. Serve it with grilled vegetables (page 92) and lavash bread.

2 (15-ounce) cans cannellini or Great Northern beans, drained and rinsed

2 tablespoons extra-virgin olive oil

$^{1}/_{4}$ cup lemon juice

$^{1}/_{4}$ teaspoon ground turmeric

$^{1}/_{2}$ teaspoon ground cumin

$^{1}/_{8}$ teaspoon ground ginger

$^{1}/_{8}$ teaspoon ground cinnamon

$^{1}/_{4}$ cup pomegranate seeds (optional)

Ground sweet paprika for garnish

Place the beans in the bowl of a food processor and pulse until a thick paste is formed.

In a small bowl, whisk together the oil, lemon juice, turmeric, cumin, ginger, and cinnamon. With the motor running, add this mixture to the food processor, scraping down the sides as necessary, until a smooth, creamy spread is formed. If the mixture is too thick, add up to $^{1}/_{4}$ cup water 1 tablespoon at a time. Transfer to a bowl, cover, and chill for at least 2 hours.

Serve chilled or at room temperature, garnished with the pomegranate seeds, if using, and a sprinkling of paprika. This dip will keep tightly covered in the refrigerator for up to 10 days.

MAKES 3 CUPS (24 SERVINGS)
Per serving: 40 calories (29% from fat), fat: 1.2g, carbohydrates: 5.5g, protein: 1.47g

Creamy Dips
and Spreads

Sesame-Tofu Dip

Tahini is made from ground sesame seeds. It is very high in fat but very flavorful, so a little goes a long way. Serve this with an assortment of flatbreads, such as pita, lavash, and roti.

12 ounces low-fat soft tofu
1/4 cup nonfat sour cream
1 tablespoon tahini (sesame paste)
2 drops of toasted sesame oil

1 teaspoon sugar
1/2 teaspoon salt
1 tablespoon soy sauce
1 tablespoon white wine vinegar

Place the tofu in a fine-mesh strainer. Press down and squeeze out any excess moisture until reduced to about 1 cup.

Place the tofu in a food processor along with the sour cream, tahini, sesame oil, sugar, salt, soy sauce, and vinegar. Process until smooth. Transfer to a bowl, cover, and chill.

MAKES 1 1/2 CUPS (12 SERVINGS)
Per serving: 37 calories (30% from fat), fat: 1.2g, carbohydrates: 5g, protein: 1.55g

Honey-Mustard Pretzel Dip

This is the ultimate pretzel mustard—tangy, spicy, sweet, and crunchy! It is also great served with crisp bagel chips or a selection of crudités such as cauliflower, carrots, broccoli, and jicama.

1/2 cup honey
3/4 cup whole-grain mustard
1/4 teaspoon turmeric

1/8 teaspoon ground ginger
2 to 3 tablespoons finely ground dry bread crumbs

In a small bowl, combine the honey, mustard, turmeric, and ginger. Add the bread crumbs 1 tablespoon at a time, blending well after each addition. Let the dip stand for 5 minutes after the second tablespoonful is added; it will thicken as it stands. If it is still too thin, add the remaining bread crumbs. Serve at room temperature.

MAKES 1 ¼ CUPS (10 SERVINGS)
Per serving: 77 calories (1% from fat), fat: 0.1g, carbohydrates: 15.5g, protein: 0.47g

Blue Cheese and Brandy Spread

Calvados is a wonderful apple brandy from the Normandy region of France. It pairs beautifully with the sharp bite of the blue cheese. Regular brandy can also be used. Serve this with crisp apple wedges and perhaps a sip of that brandy!

½ cup applesauce
1 cup nonfat cream cheese
2 tablespoons Calvados,
   apple brandy, or regular
   brandy

¼ cup crumbled blue cheese
Salt and black pepper

Place the applesauce and the cream cheese in a food processor and pulse until smooth. Transfer to a bowl and blend in the Calvados and blue cheese. Season to taste with salt and pepper. Transfer to a bowl, cover, and chill for at least 1 hour. This is best served the same day it is made chilled or at room temperature.

MAKES 1 ¾ CUPS (14 SERVINGS)
Per serving: 37 calories (17% from fat), fat: 0.7g, carbohydrates: 3g, protein: 3.38g

Velvety Roasted Garlic and Romano Dip

This dip's richness comes from the roasted garlic and the small amount of very flavorful cheese. Go ahead and indulge! A delicious way to serve this is with steamed artichoke leaves.

5 to 6 heads of garlic,
  roasted (page 17) and
  cooled
3 tablespoons nonfat
  mayonnaise

2 tablespoons grated Romano
  cheese
Salt and black pepper

Squeeze the pulp out of the cooled heads of garlic. You should have approximately ¾ cup. Blend the garlic puree, mayonnaise, and Romano cheese together in a small bowl. Cover and chill for at least 1 hour. Let sit at room temperature for at least 15 minutes before serving. Season to taste with salt and pepper.

MAKES 1 CUP (8 SERVINGS)
Per serving: 43 calories (11% from fat), fat: 0.5g, carbohydrates: 8.1g, protein: 1.84g

Creamy Apricot Curry Dip

This delicious, simple dip is a great way to use any leftover chutney. It is wonderful served with Chicken Satay (page 86).

¾ cup Curried Apricot
  Chutney (page 50)
  or store-bought chutney

1 cup skim milk

Combine the chutney and milk in the bowl of a food processor and process until smooth. Serve immediately or chill. This dip will keep several days tightly covered and refrigerated.

MAKES 1 ½ CUPS (12 SERVINGS)
Per serving: 30 calories (2% from fat), fat: 0.08g, carbohydrates: 6.89g, protein: 0.94g

Roasted Garlic and Tofu Spread

The simplicity of this dip makes it extremely versatile. It is equally delicious paired with vegetables or crackers, or even spread on a sandwich.

*3 to 4 heads of garlic, roasted
(page 17) and cooled
12 ounces low-fat soft tofu
1 tablespoon chopped fresh
parsley*

*1 teaspoon salt
¼ teaspoon curry powder
½ tablespoon lemon juice*

Squeeze the pulp out of the heads of garlic. You should have approximately ½ cup of pulp.

Place the tofu in a fine-mesh strainer. Press down and squeeze out the excess moisture until the tofu is reduced to 1 cup.

Place the tofu, garlic pulp, parsley, salt, curry powder, and lemon juice in a food processor and process until smooth. Transfer to a bowl, cover, and chill for at least 1 hour. Serve chilled or at room temperature.

MAKES 1 ½ CUPS (12 SERVINGS)
Per serving: 42 calories (26% from fat), fat: 1.32g, carbohydrates: 4.45g, protein: 3.73g

Nonfat Yogurt Cheese

Yogurt cheese is an extremely versatile ingredient used in several recipes here. It is also quite tasty on its own or drizzled with a little honey. A traditional Lebanese breakfast consists of yogurt cheese spread on a flat, pitalike bread and sprinkled with a spice mixture called zataar, which consists of sumac, thyme, sesame seeds, and pepper. In addition to making cheese with plain yogurt, blended flavored yogurts can be used. These make great, healthy breakfast spreads for muffins, bagels, or slices of fresh fruit.

The cheese will keep, tightly covered and refrigerated, for up to one week.

32 ounces plain nonfat yogurt, preferably an
all-natural brand with active cultures

Place the yogurt in a fine-mesh strainer lined with a double layer of cheesecloth. Place over a bowl, cover with plastic wrap, and refrigerate for 12 to 24 hours until the yogurt has a thick, cream cheese–like consistency. Discard the liquid and use the cheese for the desired recipe or in one of the following variations.

MAKES 1 1/2 CUPS (12 SERVINGS)
Per serving: 42 calories (3% from fat), fat: 0.1g, carbohydrates: 5.8g, protein: 4.33g

Variations. *Fresh Fruit or Jam:* Blend in chopped or pureed strawberries, raspberries, peaches, plums, or your favorite type of jam or preserves. Serve with pancakes or waffles.

Citrus: Blend in freshly squeezed orange juice and a bit of orange or lemon zest. Serve spread on biscotti.

Apple Cinnamon: Blend in applesauce, cinnamon, and a sprinkling of sugar. Serve spread on whole grain toast.

Fines Herbes: Blend in chopped fresh chervil, parsley, tarragon, and chives. This makes a great omelet filling.

Indian Curry: Blend in curry powder, raisins, and finely chopped almonds. Serve with pita bread or lavash, or along with Chicken Satay (page 86).

Ricotta and Chive Dip

This traditional favorite is given extra zip with the addition of spicy radishes, and a calorie and fat makeover by using low-fat instead of whole milk ricotta cheese. Serve with lots of crisp, fresh vegetables, such as thin slices of fennel, sugar snap peas, cherry tomatoes, and blanched asparagus spears.

This dip is best served the same day it is made.

1 cup low-fat ricotta cheese	*2 tablespoons chopped fresh*
1/2 cup minced chives	* parsley*
1/2 cup finely chopped	*2 teaspoons lemon juice*
* radishes*	*Salt and white pepper*
1/2 teaspoon salt	

Puree the ricotta cheese in a food processor until smooth and creamy. Transfer to a bowl and add the chives, radishes, salt, parsley, and lemon juice. Season to taste with salt and pepper. Stir to combine, cover, and chill at least 1 hour.

MAKES 1 1/2 CUPS (12 SERVINGS)
Per serving: 22 calories (30% from fat), fat: 0.6g, carbohydrates: 1.3g, protein: 2.14g

Crunchy Creamy
Water Chestnut–Scallion Dip

I love the crisp crunch of water chestnuts! This is a great party dip—with all sorts of raw or lightly blanched veggies, as well as with chilled cooked shrimp—that can be made all in one bowl a day ahead.

1 cup Nonfat Yogurt Cheese (page 40)
1/2 cup low-fat mayonnaise
1 small onion, finely chopped
8 to 12 canned water chestnuts, drained and chopped (about 1/2 cup)

4 scallions, white and green parts, finely chopped (about 1/2 cup)
1/2 teaspoon salt
Freshly ground black pepper
1/2 teaspoon dill weed
1 teaspoon lemon juice

Blend together the yogurt cheese, mayonnaise, onion, water chestnuts, scallions, salt, pepper to taste, dill weed, and lemon juice. Cover and chill for at least 1 hour and up to 24 hours.

MAKES 2 CUPS (16 SERVINGS)
Per serving: 41 calories (25% from fat), fat: 1.09g, carbohydrates: 4.9g, protein: 2.56g

Horseradish-Dijon Dip

*D*ifferent brands of prepared horseradish vary greatly in their strength, so I have given a range for the amount. Add the smaller amount and then taste to see if you want more.

Try serving this spicy dip with matzoh, pretzels, and slices of cocktail rye bread. This dip will keep for up to 10 days refrigerated.

½ cup Dijon mustard
⅓ cup nonfat mayonnaise
2 to 3 tablespoons prepared
  horseradish

1 tablespoon light brown
  sugar
½ teaspoon soy sauce
Dash of Tabasco sauce

In a small bowl, combine the mustard, mayonnaise, horseradish, brown sugar, soy sauce, and Tabasco sauce. Cover and chill.

MAKES 1 CUP (8 SERVINGS)
Per serving: 28 calories (23% from fat), fat: 0.7g, carbohydrates: 4.66g, protein: 0.83g

Taramasalata

*T*aramasalata is a Greek spread that traditionally is mostly oil. This version is considerably lighter, but it still has the rich, salty fish roe flavor plus a spicy zing. The bread called for in the recipe acts as a thickener, making the spread surprisingly smooth and light. Serve this pretty pink dip with warm pita bread, olives, and cucumber sticks.

8 slices firm white bread,
  crusts removed
1 garlic clove, minced
½ cup nonfat yogurt

½ cup nonfat sour cream
2 ounces red lumpfish roe
2 tablespoons lemon juice
1 teaspoon sugar

Tear the bread into pieces and place in a food processor. Pulse until fine crumbs are formed. Add the garlic, yogurt, sour cream, and roe and pulse until smooth. Transfer the mixture to a bowl and stir in the lemon juice and sugar. Cover and refrigerate until serving.

MAKES 1 ½ CUPS (12 SERVINGS)
Per serving: 74 calories (19% from fat), fat: 1.5g, carbohydrates: 11g, protein: 3.69g

Anchoiade

*F*or anchovy lovers only! Serve on crostini (page 90) with a little diced tomato and red onion.

3 (2-ounce) cans anchovies
25 garlic cloves, unpeeled
4 slices firm-textured white bread, crusts removed
1 cup loosely packed fresh basil leaves

1 tablespoon red wine vinegar
2 tablespoons white wine
Freshly ground black pepper (optional)

Drain the anchovies and place them in a small bowl. Cover with hot water and soak for 30 minutes, changing the water once halfway through. Drain well and spread the anchovies in a single layer on a double thickness of paper toweling. Cover with another layer of paper towels and let dry.

Place the garlic cloves in a small saucepan and cover with water. Bring to a boil over medium-high heat, reduce the heat to medium, and simmer for 15 minutes. Drain and allow to cool slightly. When cool enough to handle, peel off the skins.

Place the anchovies, garlic, bread, and basil leaves in the bowl of a food processor. Process until a smooth paste is formed. Add the vinegar and wine and pulse until combined. Taste and add a few grinds of pepper, if desired. Serve chilled or at room temperature.

MAKES 1 1/4 CUPS (10 SERVINGS)
Per serving: 87 calories (23% from fat), fat: 2.21g, carbohydrates: 9.52g, protein: 6.69g

Shrimp Cocktail Dip

Cocktail sauce and cooked shrimp blended together give the flavor of a traditional shrimp cocktail in the form of a dip. To make your own cocktail sauce, blend together $\frac{1}{2}$ cup catsup, 1 to 2 tablespoons prepared horseradish, juice of $\frac{1}{2}$ lemon, and a dash of Tabasco sauce. Serve this dip on crostini or with crudités such as bell pepper strips, button mushrooms, endive leaves, and scallions.

1 cup low-fat cottage cheese
1 (4$\frac{1}{4}$-ounce) can shrimp,
  drained
Grated zest and juice of
  $\frac{1}{2}$ lemon
1 tablespoon chopped fresh
  parsley

1$\frac{1}{2}$ tablespoons seafood
  cocktail sauce
Dash of Tabasco sauce
Salt and white pepper

In a food processor, puree the cottage cheese until smooth. Add the shrimp and pulse several times until incorporated and chopped but still somewhat chunky. Transfer to a bowl and blend in the lemon zest and juice, parsley, cocktail sauce, and Tabasco sauce. Season to taste with salt and pepper. Cover and chill at least 1 hour. This is best served the same day it is prepared.

MAKES 1 $\frac{1}{2}$ CUPS (12 SERVINGS)
Per serving: 29 calories (14% from fat), fat: 0.46g, carbohydrates: 1.49g, protein: 4.8g

Tzatziki

*I*n Greece, tzatziki is traditionally served with a selection of other dips and appetizers. This cucumber and yogurt dip is a nice accompaniment to spicy foods as it is naturally cooling and refreshing. Try serving it along with Hummus (page 29), Taramasalata (page 43), and Eggplant Caviar (page 14). The longer it sits, the stronger the garlic becomes, so if you like a mild flavor, prepare it close to the time it will be served or go easy on the garlic.

2 cucumbers	*$^1/_8$ teaspoon cayenne*
1 teaspoon kosher or sea salt	*$^3/_4$ cup plain nonfat yogurt*
1 garlic clove, minced	*$^1/_2$ cup nonfat sour cream*
Juice of $^1/_2$ lemon	*Salt and black pepper*

Peel the cucumbers and cut them in half lengthwise. With a teaspoon, scrape out all of the seeds from the center of each half. Chop each half into 1-inch chunks.

Place the cucumbers in a food processor and pulse a few times until finely chopped but not pureed. Turn the cucumbers into a colander set over a bowl and sprinkle with the salt. Cover the surface with plastic wrap and then place a weight such as a plate on top of the cucumbers. Let stand for 30 minutes.

In another bowl, combine the garlic, lemon juice, cayenne, yogurt, and sour cream. When the cucumbers have drained, add them to the bowl and mix well. Cover and chill for at least 4 hours and up to 24 hours. Add salt and pepper to taste, if desired.

MAKES 2 CUPS (16 SERVINGS)
Per serving: 20 calories (6% from fat), fat: 0.14g, carbohydrates: 3.4g, protein: 1.42g

Chutneys and Salsas

Papaya and Cilantro Salsa

This salsa, one of my favorites, is crunchy and refreshing yet has a bite. Splurge and bump up the fat just a little by sprinkling it with a few chopped roasted peanuts. This is good served with crackers, flatbread, or baked tortilla chips. A lovely canape would be a crisp toast round topped with a thin slice of smoked salmon and a dollop of papaya salsa. It is also delicious with grilled fish or chicken.

1 medium papaya
1 medium cucumber
1/4 cup chopped fresh cilantro
1 red bell pepper, seeded and diced 1/4 inch
1/2 cup diced red onion
2 scallions, white and green parts, finely chopped

1/2 teaspoon salt
1 teaspoon sugar
Juice of 1 lime
1 1/2 teaspoons lime zest
1 jalapeño pepper, seeded and minced
Freshly ground black pepper (optional)

Cut the papaya in half lengthwise and scoop out the seeds with a spoon. Remove the peel with a paring knife and cut the pulp into 1/4-inch dice. Discard the seeds and skin and place the diced papaya in a bowl. Peel the cucumber and cut in half lengthwise. With a teaspoon, scrape out the seeds from the center of each half and discard. Cut the cucumber into 1/4-inch dice and add it to the papaya. Add the cilantro, bell pepper, red onion, scallions, salt, sugar, lime juice, lime zest, and jalapeño pepper. Toss to combine and season with black pepper, if desired. Cover and chill at least 30 minutes. This salsa is best if served within a few hours of preparing.

MAKES 3 CUPS (24 SERVINGS)
Per serving: 10 calories (4% from fat), fat: 0.05g, carbohydrates: 2.44g, protein: 0.26g

Plum Tomato and Mint Salsa

*I*n this recipe, I like to use scissors, rather than a knife, to snip the herbs. This prevents the herbs from bruising and keeps the clean, light texture of this refreshing summertime salsa. A great way to serve this is as a topping for bruschetta. Cut a loaf of French bread into slices ½ inch thick. Coat lightly with olive oil spray and toast on both sides until golden. Rub the toasts with a half clove of garlic. Discard the garlic clove and top each toast with a generous spoonful of the salsa.

1¼ pounds ripe plum tomatoes, seeded and diced ¼ inch (about 3 cups)
½ cup snipped fresh mint leaves
½ cup snipped fresh basil leaves

2 tablespoons snipped fresh parsley
Finely grated zest and juice of 1 lemon
1 garlic clove, minced
½ teaspoon sugar
Salt and black pepper

In a medium bowl, toss the tomatoes with the mint leaves, basil leaves, parsley, lemon zest and juice, garlic, and sugar. Cover and chill, if desired. Season with salt and pepper to taste.

MAKES 3 CUPS (24 SERVINGS)
Per serving: 14 calories (9% from fat), fat: 0.16g, carbohydrates: 2.7g, protein: 8.6g

Curried Apricot Chutney

This sweet, tart, and spicy chutney is a great accompaniment to grilled chicken or pork tenderloin. It is also a delicious addition to tuna or chicken salad. If you have leftover chutney, make the Creamy Apricot Curry Dip on page 38.

1/2 pound dried apricots, diced 1/4 inch (about 1 1/2 cups)
1 medium onion, finely chopped
1/2 cup raisins, coarsely chopped
1 garlic clove, minced
1/2 lemon, seeds removed

1 tablespoon minced peeled fresh ginger
1/2 cup light brown sugar
2/3 cup white wine vinegar
1/3 cup frozen apple juice concentrate
1/3 cup water
1 tablespoon curry powder

Combine the apricots, onion, raisins, garlic, lemon, ginger, brown sugar, vinegar, apple juice concentrate, water, and curry powder in a nonreactive saucepan. Bring to a boil over medium heat, stirring often. Reduce the heat and simmer for 30 to 40 minutes, stirring occasionally, until the mixture is thick and the apricots are soft. Remove the lemon half, squeezing out the liquid, and let the chutney stand at room temperature until cool. Serve at once, or if refrigerating, allow to come to room temperature before serving. This will keep for 2 weeks tightly covered in the refrigerator or up to 3 months in the freezer.

MAKES 2 CUPS (16 SERVINGS)
Per serving: 88 calories: (2% from fat), fat: 0.19g, carbohydrates: 22.3g, protein: 0.94g

Citrus and Shallot Relish

*T*he tartness of this relish is a wonderful accompaniment to oysters and clams on the half shell, as well as a perfect dip for chilled shrimp and crab claws.

3/4 cup fresh lime juice
1/2 cup fresh lemon juice
1/4 cup grated peeled fresh ginger
1 tablespoon minced garlic
1/4 cup honey

2 lemons
2 limes
1 cup thinly sliced shallots
1/2 cup coarsely chopped cilantro leaves

In a nonreactive saucepan, combine the lime juice, lemon juice, ginger, garlic, and honey. Simmer over medium heat until reduced by half, about 8 minutes.

Using a vegetable or paring knife, remove the zest from the lemons and limes in long strips. Scrape off any white pith from the fruit and zest. Slice the zest into long, thin julienne strips. Seed and coarsely chop the remaining pulp. When the juice mixture has reduced, stir in the zests, pulps, and shallots. Simmer until thick, about 5 minutes more. Cool to room temperature and stir in the cilantro. Cover and chill for at least 4 hours or overnight.

MAKES 1 CUP (8 SERVINGS)
Per serving: 73 calories (2% from fat), fat: 0.19g, carbohydrates: 20.7g, protein: 1.22g

Summer Garden Herb Salsa

This is best made in late summer when zucchini, tomatoes, and corn are in seasonal abundance. I find that summer corn needs almost no cooking, so I place it in a colander and simply pour boiling water over it. Here, just drain the cooked vegetables over the corn and you save a step. This method works with frozen corn, too.

This salsa is a great complement to just about anything cooked on the grill. Try grilling thick slices of bread rubbed with just a touch of fragrant extra-virgin olive oil and topping them with the salsa.

1 large zucchini, diced $^1/_4$ inch
1 medium yellow squash, diced $^1/_4$ inch
1 cup corn kernels, fresh or frozen and defrosted
1 cucumber
2 large tomatoes, seeded and diced $^1/_4$ inch
$^1/_3$ cup chopped fresh basil
$^1/_4$ cup chopped fresh parsley
1 tablespoon chopped fresh thyme
2 tablespoons white wine vinegar
1 tablespoon Dijon mustard
1 teaspoon Worcestershire sauce
1 teaspoon sugar
Salt and black pepper

Bring a large saucepan of salted water to a boil. Add the diced zucchini and yellow squash and cook for 2 minutes. Place the corn kernels in a colander and pour the cooked zucchini and squash over it to drain. Rinse the vegetables with cold running water and drain well.

Peel the cucumber and cut in half lengthwise. Using a teaspoon, scrape the seeds out of the center of each half. Discard the seeds and dice the cucumber into $^1/_4$-inch cubes.

In a large bowl, combine the cucumber, tomatoes, basil, parsley, and thyme. Add the drained cooked vegetables.

In a small bowl, whisk together the vinegar, mustard, Worcestershire sauce, and sugar. Pour over the vegetables and toss to combine well. Season with salt and pepper to taste, cover, and chill for at least 1 hour. This salsa is best served within 1 day of preparing.

MAKES 5 CUPS (40 SERVINGS)
Per serving: 9 calories (12% from fat), fat: 0.13g, carbohydrates: 1.86g, protein: 0.11g

Tequila Pico de Gallo

There are many recipes for pico de gallo, which translates inexplicably to "rooster's beak," but is more commonly known as salsa. This one contains tequila, which gives it an unusual, lively kick.

1 medium cucumber
1 large tomato, seeded and
* diced*
1 cup diced red onion
1/4 cup chopped fresh cilantro

1 jalapeño pepper, seeded
* and chopped*
Juice of 1/2 lime
2 tablespoons tequila
Salt and black pepper

Peel the cucumber and cut in half lengthwise. With a teaspoon, scrape out the seeds from the center of each half. Discard the seeds and chop the cucumber into small dice.

In a large bowl, combine the cucumber, tomato, red onion, cilantro, jalapeño pepper, lime juice, and tequila. Toss to combine well. Season to taste with salt and pepper. Cover and chill for at least 1 hour. The pico de gallo can be made up to a day ahead.

MAKES 3 CUPS (24 SERVINGS)
Per serving: 9 calories (5% from fat), fat: 0.05g, carbohydrates: 1.39g, protein: 0.23g

Vidalia Onion and Apple Chutney

Sweet Vidalia onions, tart crisp apples, and aromatic spices combine to make a delicious savory chutney.

A lovely and unusual way to serve this chutney would be with a platter of Chicken Satay (page 86) surrounded with fresh fig halves and apple wedges.

2 large Vidalia onions, quartered and thinly sliced (about 5 cups)
4 tart apples, such as Granny Smith, cored, peeled, and chopped (about 4 cups)
Juice and chopped seeded pulp of 1 lemon
1 cup chopped dates
1 cup firmly packed light brown sugar
$^3/_4$ cup apple juice
$^3/_4$ cup apple cider vinegar
2 garlic cloves, minced
1 tablespoon chopped peeled fresh ginger
1 (3-inch) piece cinnamon stick
1 tablespoon mustard seeds
1 tablespoon fennel seeds
$^1/_2$ tablespoon caraway seeds

In a large nonreactive saucepan, combine the onions, apples, lemon juice and pulp, dates, brown sugar, apple juice, vinegar, garlic, ginger, cinnamon stick, mustard seeds, fennel seeds, and caraway seeds. Bring to a boil over medium-high heat, stirring occasionally. Reduce the heat and simmer 40 to 45 minutes, stirring occasionally, until the liquid is mostly reduced and the mixture is thick. Cool at room temperature. Serve warm or chilled. The chutney will keep tightly covered in the refrigerator for up to 2 weeks or 3 months in the freezer.

MAKES 4 CUPS (32 SERVINGS)
Per serving: 52 calories (4% from fat), fat: 0.24g, carbohydrates: 13.19g, protein: 0.4g

Savory Cranberry Chutney

Here's a spicy, sweet-tart accompaniment that shouldn't be saved for Thanksgiving. Try serving an appetizer of crostini topped with thin slices of smoked turkey and a dollop of this unusual chutney.

3 cups cranberries
1 apple, cored and diced
  $1/4$ inch
1 medium onion, diced
  $1/4$ inch
1 orange, zested, peeled, and
  pulp seeded and chopped
$1/2$ cup raisins
$1/2$ cup sugar
$1/4$ teaspoon ground cloves

$1/4$ teaspoon ground allspice
$1/4$ teaspoon ground ginger
$1/2$ teaspoon fennel seeds
1 tablespoon chopped fresh
  savory or parsley
1 tablespoon chopped fresh
  thyme
$1/2$ cup balsamic vinegar
$1/2$ cup white wine

Combine the cranberries, apple, onion, orange zest and pulp, raisins, sugar, cloves, allspice, ginger, fennel, savory, thyme, vinegar, and wine in a nonreactive saucepan and bring to a boil over medium heat. Reduce the heat and simmer, stirring often, for 25 minutes, until thickened to the consistency of a stew. It will still be somewhat liquidy, but it will set up as it cools. Allow to cool to room temperature, transfer to a bowl, and serve at room temperature or chilled. This chutney will keep for up to 2 weeks tightly covered in the refrigerator or 3 months in the freezer.

MAKES 4 CUPS (32 SERVINGS)
Per serving: 36 calories (2% from fat), fat: 0.07, carbohydrates: 8.5g, protein: 0.23g

Tomatillo and Avocado Salsa

Tomatillos look like little green tomatoes with a brown, papery outer husk. They have a tart lemony flavor that is intensified by toasting or roasting. Look for tomatillos that are firm and green with close-fitting husks.

Serve this spicy salsa with lots of crisp baked tortilla chips (page 84).

1½ pounds tomatillos (about 20)
½ small Hass avocado, diced ½ inch
2 to 3 jalapeño peppers, seeded and minced

¾ cup minced red onion
⅓ cup chopped fresh cilantro
Zest and juice of ½ lime
1 tablespoon sugar
Salt and black pepper

Remove the husks from the tomatillos and rinse well. Heat a cast-iron skillet or grill over high heat until smoking hot. Add the tomatillos and cook, turning frequently with tongs, until lightly charred on all sides, about 10 minutes. Remove to a bowl and allow to cool slightly.

When cool enough to handle, cut the tomatillos in half and place in the bowl of a food processor. Pulse several times until coarsely chopped but not pureed.

In a bowl, toss the tomatillos with the avocado, jalapeño peppers, red onion, cilantro, lime zest and juice, and sugar. Season to taste with salt and pepper. Cover and chill for at least 1 hour. This salsa is best served within a few hours of preparing it.

MAKES 2½ CUPS (20 SERVINGS)
Per serving: 25 calories (30% from fat), fat: 0.86g, carbohydrates: 3.85g, protein: 0.5g

Hot Dips

Bubbly Baked Pizza Dip

*A*ll the goodness of hot, cheesy pizza is in this dip, one of those luscious concoctions you were afraid you'd have to give up forever. It can be assembled up to a day ahead, refrigerated, and then baked just before serving (let it come to room temperature before popping it in the oven). Served with a salad and lots of crusty Italian bread, this can be a meal!

1 medium onion, chopped
2 garlic cloves, minced
4 ounces lean Italian turkey sausage
³/₄ cup nonfat cream cheese
¹/₂ cup nonfat sour cream
1 teaspoon dried oregano
3 tablespoons dried bread crumbs

³/₄ cup nonfat marinara sauce
3 tablespoons sliced black olives
³/₄ cup shredded low-fat mozzarella cheese
Dash of red pepper flakes

Preheat the oven to 400°F. and lightly coat a nonstick skillet with nonstick cooking spray. Add the onions and garlic and sauté 3 to 4 minutes over medium heat, until soft and golden. Slide the sausage out of its casing and add to the skillet. Sauté, breaking the sausage up with a fork, for 6 to 7 minutes, until thoroughly cooked.

In a bowl, blend the cream cheese, sour cream, and oregano until smooth. Spread this mixture on the bottom of a round cake pan, pie plate, or shallow casserole. Sprinkle 1¹/₂ tablespoons of the bread crumbs over this. Spread with the marinara sauce, then the sausage mixture. Sprinkle with the olives and remaining bread crumbs. Top with the mozzarella cheese and a dash or two of red pepper flakes.

Bake for 15 to 20 minutes, until hot and bubbly and the cheese is melted and just beginning to brown. Serve at once.

MAKES 3 1/2 CUPS (28 SERVINGS)
Per serving: 36 calories (30% from fat), fat: 1.23g, carbohydrates: 3.13g, protein: 3.04g

Creamy Baked Clam Dip

*T*his hot, creamy, cheesy clam dip is always popular. It goes well with breadsticks or cocktail rye and pumpernickel breads, as well as with vegetables such as endive, celery, and zucchini.

1/2 cup nonfat cream cheese	*Dash of Tabasco sauce*
1/2 cup nonfat sour cream	*1 teaspoon Worcestershire*
1/2 cup grated low-fat	*sauce*
Cheddar cheese	*1 tablespoon chopped fresh*
1 garlic clove, minced	*parsley*
1 shallot, minced	*1 (7-ounce) can clams*
Juice of 1/2 lemon	*Salt and white pepper*

Preheat the oven to 350°F.

In a medium-sized bowl, blend together the cream cheese and sour cream until smooth. Stir in the Cheddar cheese, garlic, and shallot. Add the lemon juice, Tabasco sauce, Worcestershire sauce, parsley, and clams with their juice. Season to taste with salt and pepper.

Pour into a 2-cup ovenproof ramekin or pie plate and bake for 20 minutes, until hot and bubbly and the Cheddar cheese is melted. Remove from the oven, stir well, and serve immediately.

MAKES 2 CUPS (16 SERVINGS)
Per serving: 36 calories (20% from fat), fat: 0.75g, carbohydrates: 2.58g, protein: 4.45g

Tomato Fondue

You know how everybody loves to sop up their pasta sauce with their bread? Well, here is a hot fondue that lets them do just that! It is also great with breadsticks or Sirloin or Chicken Satay (page 86).

1 medium onion, finely chopped	1/4 cup cold water
1 cup red wine	1 cup diced fresh tomatoes
1 (28-ounce) can crushed tomatoes	2 anchovies, rinsed and finely chopped (optional)
2 bay leaves	Salt and black pepper
1 tablespoon sugar	2 tablespoons grated Parmesan cheese
2 teaspoons chopped fresh thyme or 1 teaspoon dried	Chopped fresh parsley for garnish
2 tablespoons cornstarch	

Lightly coat a large saucepan or Dutch oven with nonstick cooking spray. Add the onions and sauté over medium heat for 2 to 3 minutes, until they just begin to color. Add the wine, crushed tomatoes, and bay leaves and simmer 10 minutes, until slightly thickened. Stir in the sugar and thyme.

In a small cup, dissolve the cornstarch in the water. Add to the tomato mixture and simmer, stirring, 1 to 2 minutes, until thickened and glossy. Stir in the diced tomatoes and anchovies, if using. Season with salt and pepper to taste. Transfer to a fondue pot or keep warm for serving. Sprinkle with grated Parmesan cheese and chopped fresh parsley and serve with chunks of crusty Italian bread.

MAKES 4 CUPS (32 SERVINGS)
Per serving: 20 calories (12% from fat), fat: 0.27g, carbohydrates: 2.83g, protein: 0.55g

Baked Artichoke Dip

This party favorite has been considerably lightened up here, but it still has that rich creamy texture people love. It can be assembled ahead of time and baked at the last minute.

Serve this dip with crackers, bagel chips, or pita bread.

$^3/_4$ cup nonfat cottage cheese
$^1/_2$ cup nonfat mayonnaise
1 garlic clove
1 (10-ounce) package frozen
   artichoke hearts, defrosted

Juice of $^1/_2$ lemon
4 tablespoons grated
   Parmesan cheese
Salt and black pepper

Preheat the oven to 400°F.

In a food processor, combine the cottage cheese, mayonnaise, and garlic and process until smooth. Transfer to a bowl. Coarsely chop the artichoke hearts and add them to the cottage cheese mixture along with the lemon juice and 3 tablespoons of the Parmesan cheese. Season to taste with salt and pepper and stir to combine.

Lightly coat a shallow ovenproof casserole or pie plate with non-stick cooking spray and spread the dip in the pan. Sprinkle with the remaining tablespoon Parmesan cheese and place in the preheated oven. Bake for 15 minutes, until hot and bubbly. Place under the broiler for 1 to 2 minutes, until the top is lightly browned, and serve at once.

MAKES 2 $^1/_2$ CUPS (20 SERVINGS)
Per serving: 23 calories (18% from fat), fat: 0.44g, carbohydrates: 2.63g, protein: 2.1g

Tex-Mex Mole Dip

This hearty dip combined with some flour tortillas could be the centerpiece of a casual meal. It calls for a couple of unusual ingredients. Epazote, an herb used in many Mexican dishes, has a distinctive, spicy, slightly soapy flavor. It is available in the ethnic section of some supermarkets. If you cannot find it, oregano can be substituted. The addition of cocoa may seem strange, but chocolate is a traditional ingredient in mole poblano. The combination of the cocoa and the tomato sauce is rich and woodsy, not at all chocolaty.

2 cups chicken broth
1 cup water
2 boneless, skinless chicken breast halves (about 5 ounces each)
1 (15-ounce) can kidney beans, drained and rinsed
1/2 cup chopped onion
1 teaspoon chili powder
1/2 teaspoon dried epazote
1 teaspoon unsweetened cocoa powder

2/3 cup tomato sauce
1 tablespoon tomato paste
1 1/2 cups chopped fresh tomatoes
2 tablespoons chopped fresh cilantro
2 jalapeño peppers, seeded and chopped
1/2 cup grated low-fat Monterey Jack cheese

In a medium saucepan, combine the chicken broth with the water and bring to a boil. Add the chicken breasts, cover, and reduce the heat to medium-low. Poach for 8 to 10 minutes, until the chicken is cooked through. Remove from the liquid and allow to cool slightly. Finely shred the chicken.

Preheat the oven to 400°F. Place the beans in the bowl of a food processor and process until smooth. Lightly coat a large skillet with nonstick cooking spray. Add the onion and sauté over medium heat until soft and lightly browned, 5 to 6 minutes. Add the chili powder, epazote, and cocoa powder and stir to combine. Add the tomato sauce and tomato paste and cook, stirring, for 2 to 3 minutes. Stir in the pureed beans.

Lightly coat a shallow ovenproof casserole or a 10-inch pie or cake plate with nonstick spray. Spoon the bean mixture into the pan, spreading evenly over the bottom. Layer the shredded chicken over the beans.

In a bowl, toss the tomatoes with the cilantro and jalapeño peppers. Spoon this mixture evenly over the chicken. Sprinkle the cheese over all. Place in the oven and bake for 20 minutes, until the cheese is melted and the dip is hot and bubbly. Serve at once.

MAKES ABOUT 5 CUPS (40 SERVINGS)
Per serving: 26 calories (17% from fat), fat: 0.47g, carbohydrates: 2.64g, protein: 2.68g

Toasted Corn Soufflé Dip

*T*his soufflé could also be served as a side dish, but it makes a surprisingly yummy dip as well, served with toasty garlic-rubbed bread.

$^1/_2$ cup finely chopped onion	Dash of cayenne
$^1/_2$ teaspoon dried thyme	2 large eggs, separated
2 cups corn kernels, fresh or frozen and defrosted	$^1/_2$ cup skim milk
1 cup nonfat cottage cheese	Salt and black pepper
Dash of grated nutmeg	$^1/_4$ cup grated Romano cheese
	2 large egg whites

Preheat the oven to 325°F. and lightly coat a 1$^1/_2$-quart casserole with nonstick cooking spray and set aside.

Lightly coat a nonstick skillet with nonstick cooking spray. Add the onions and thyme and sauté over medium heat, until lightly browned, about 5 minutes. Transfer to a bowl and wipe the skillet clean. Heat the skillet over high heat. Add 1 cup corn and toss until golden, 2 to 3 minutes. Add the corn to the onion mixture and let cool.

In a food processor, combine the remaining cup of corn, cottage cheese, nutmeg, cayenne, egg yolks, and milk. Season with salt and pepper and process until smooth. Blend into the cooled corn and onion mixture and stir in 3 tablespoons of the Romano cheese.

Whip the 4 egg whites to stiff peaks. Fold one third of the egg whites into the corn mixture. Then fold in the remaining whites. Turn into the prepared casserole and sprinkle with the remaining tablespoon Romano cheese. Bake for 1 hour, until puffed, golden brown, and a knife inserted in the center comes out damp but clean. Allow to rest for 15 minutes. The soufflé will deflate slightly as it cools.

MAKES 5 CUPS (40 SERVINGS)
Per serving: 19 calories (23% from fat), fat: 0.52g, carbohydrates: 2.06g, protein: 1.81g

Pâtés, Mousses, and Terrines

Ruby Beet Terrine

The color of this easy-to-make terrine is truly striking. Serve it on a bed of dark leafy greens for a festive presentation, and accompany with thin slices of pumpernickel, rye, and marble bread.

1 (14½-ounce) can whole
  beets, drained (reserve
  ¼ cup liquid)
¼ cup nonfat cottage cheese
¼ cup nonfat mayonnaise
¼ teaspoon dry mustard
2 teaspoons balsamic vinegar

1 tablespoon chopped fresh
  dill weed
¼ cup water
1 package unflavored gelatin
Salt and black pepper
Fresh dill sprigs for garnish

Place the beets, cottage cheese, mayonnaise, mustard, and vinegar in the bowl of a food processor and process to a smooth puree. Transfer to a bowl and stir in the dill weed.

Combine the reserved beet liquid with the water in a small saucepan. Sprinkle with the gelatin and heat over low heat, stirring, until the gelatin is dissolved.

Add the gelatin to the beet mixture, stirring to combine thoroughly. Season with salt and pepper to taste. Pour into a 2½-cup mold or bowl lined with plastic wrap. Cover and chill for at least 4 hours or overnight.

To unmold, immerse the mold to just below the rim in warm water for several seconds. Run a small sharp knife around the edges of the terrine to loosen. Invert on a serving plate and gently peel off the plastic wrap. Serve whole or sliced into individual servings, garnished with dill sprigs.

MAKES ONE 2¼-CUP TERRINE (20 SERVINGS)
Per serving: 13 calories (2% from fat), fat: 0.02g, carbohydrates: 2.23g, protein: 0.94g

Lentil and Rosemary Pâté

You would never guess this rich-tasting pâté was made from such humble ingredients! It tastes very much like chicken liver pâté, and the rosemary lends a nutty, woodsy flavor.

Serve this spread with matzoh and chunks of rye bread.

1 cup dried brown lentils
4 cups water
1 tablespoon vegetable oil
1 large onion, chopped
1½ teaspoons crumbled dried
   rosemary

2 tablespoons red wine
   vinegar
Black pepper
3 hard-boiled egg whites,
   coarsely chopped
Salt

Place the lentils in a strainer and rinse with cold running water, picking out any pebbles. Place the lentils in a saucepan with the water. Bring to a boil over high heat. Reduce the heat and simmer, uncovered, for 30 minutes, until very tender. If necessary, add more water during cooking to keep the lentils wet. Drain well.

Meanwhile, heat the oil in a large skillet and add the onions. Sauté over low heat, stirring often, for 10 minutes. Take care not to brown the onions. Add the rosemary, vinegar, and several grinds of black pepper and sauté for 10 minutes more. Stir in the cooked lentils and cook 3 to 4 minutes more.

Transfer the contents of the skillet to a food processor. Add the hard-boiled egg whites and process until a smooth, pâtélike consistency is reached. Season to taste with salt and pepper. Transfer the pâté to a serving bowl or crock and serve at room temperature or chilled. The pâté will keep refrigerated for several days.

MAKES 3 CUPS (24 SERVINGS)
Per serving: 19 calories (28% from fat), fat: 0.6g, carbohydrates: 2.4g, protein: 1.23g

Salmon Mousse

*T*his is a lovely, light mousse, ideal for a summertime lunch or brunch. If you do not have a decorative mold to chill it in, a small loaf pan or bowl will work just as well. You could even pour it into several small ramekins or tiny loaf pans for individual servings.

³/₄ cup chicken broth
1 packet unflavored gelatin
¹/₂ cup nonfat mayonnaise
1 cup nonfat sour cream
1¹/₂ tablespoons snipped fresh
  dill weed
1 shallot, minced
2 teaspoons capers, drained,
  rinsed, and chopped

¹/₂ teaspoon salt
¹/₈ teaspoon white pepper
1 (7¹/₂-ounce) can pink
  salmon, drained
Additional dill sprigs and
  capers for garnish

In a small saucepan, heat the chicken broth over medium heat until simmering. Remove from the heat, stir in the gelatin, and continue stirring until dissolved. Allow to cool to room temperature.

In a medium bowl, combine the mayonnaise, sour cream, dill weed, shallot, capers, salt, and pepper. Add the cooled gelatin mixture and blend until smooth. With a fork, break the salmon into small flakes and fold into the sour cream mixture.

Lightly spray a 3-cup mold with nonstick cooking spray or line with plastic wrap. Pour the mousse into the mold and cover tightly. Chill for 6 hours or overnight.

To unmold, dip the mold up to the rim in warm water for several seconds. Run a knife around the edges and carefully invert the mold onto a serving plate. Tap the bottom of the mold and when you hear it release, gently lift the mold off of the mousse. Peel off the plastic wrap, if used. Surround the mousse with fresh dill sprigs and garnish with additional capers.

MAKES ONE 2 1/2-CUP MOUSSE OR FIVE 1/2-CUP MOUSSES (20 SERVINGS)
Per serving: 34 calories (21% from fat), fat: 0.75g, carbohydrates: 3.19g, protein: 3.05g

Roasted Red Pepper Mousse

*A*lthough this is not technically a mousse, I like to call it that because of its lovely, light, creamy texture. If yellow bell peppers are available, try using them instead of red. They lend a milder, sweet flavor and change the color of this appetizer. Serve this light, colorful spread with garlicky crostini (page 90).

*3 large red bell peppers,
   roasted (page 20)
3/4 cup Nonfat Yogurt
   Cheese (page 40)
1/4 teaspoon dried oregano*

*1/4 teaspoon dried thyme
2 teaspoons lime juice
1/2 teaspoon sugar
Salt and black pepper*

Peel, seed, and devein the peppers and chop coarsely. Place in a food processor. Pulse until finely chopped but not pureed. Transfer to a fine-mesh strainer set over a bowl. You should have about 1 1/4 cups pulp. Press down on the peppers to release any excess liquid. Transfer the pulp to a bowl, add the yogurt cheese, and blend until smooth. Add the oregano, thyme, lime juice, and sugar. Season to taste with salt and pepper. Cover and chill at least 4 hours or overnight.

MAKES 1 1/4 CUPS (10 SERVINGS)
Per serving: 35 calories (3% from fat), fat: 0.14g, carbohydrates: 5.7g, protein: 3.13g

Three-Vegetable Terrine

*T*his beautiful vegetarian terrine is certain to impress your guests. Although time consuming, the purees can be made up to two days ahead, and the terrine can be baked one day ahead. Serve it whole at a buffet or serve individual slices as an appetizer at a seated dinner.

³/₄ pound carrots (about 4 medium), peeled and cut into 1-inch pieces
³/₄ pound cauliflower (¹/₂ a medium-sized head), trimmed and cut into florets
³/₄ pound watercress (1 large bunch)
1 cup nonfat cottage cheese
1 tablespoon light brown sugar
Squeeze of lemon juice

1 teaspoon chopped fresh thyme or ¹/₂ teaspoon dried
Salt and black pepper
¹/₂ cup low-fat buttermilk
2 teaspoons Cognac
1 teaspoon grated lemon zest
1 tablespoon chopped fresh tarragon or 1 teaspoon dried
1 teaspoon balsamic vinegar
4 large egg whites
2 whole large eggs

Line the bottom of a 9×5×3-inch loaf or terrine pan with parchment paper and coat with nonstick spray. Bring a large pot of salted water to a boil. Add the carrots and boil for 5 to 7 minutes, until very tender but still bright orange. Drain and rinse with cold water.

Meanwhile, bring another pot of salted water to a boil and add the cauliflower. Boil for 5 to 7 minutes, until tender when pierced with a fork. Drain well and rinse under cold running water.

At the same time, if you have enough pots, bring a third pot of water to a boil and add the watercress. Boil for 1 to 2 minutes, until tender but still bright green. Drain well and rinse with cold running water. Remove the leaves and discard the stems.

Preheat the oven to 350°F. In a food processor, combine the carrots with ½ cup of the cottage cheese, the brown sugar, lemon juice, and thyme. Process until smoothly pureed. Transfer to a bowl and season with salt and pepper to taste.

Clean the bowl of the food processor and combine the cauliflower and buttermilk. Process until smooth. Transfer to a bowl, stir in the Cognac and lemon zest. Add salt and pepper to taste.

Place the watercress in the cleaned bowl of the food processor along with the remaining ½ cup cottage cheese, the tarragon, and balsamic vinegar. Process until smoothly pureed. Transfer to a bowl and season with salt and pepper to taste.

In a small bowl, whisk together the egg whites and whole eggs. Divide this mixture evenly among the 3 purees, mixing each well to combine. Pour the carrot mixture into the prepared pan, smoothing with a knife. Spread the cauliflower mixture over the carrot and smooth with a knife, trying not to disturb the carrot layer underneath. Spread the watercress mixture on top, smoothing evenly with a knife, again trying not to disrupt the bottom layers.

Lightly coat a piece of aluminum foil with nonstick cooking spray and cover the pan. Place the terrine pan inside a larger baking pan and pour hot water into the baking pan so it comes halfway up the sides of the terrine. Place in the preheated oven and bake for 45 to 50 minutes. Uncover and bake for about 10 minutes more, until a knife inserted in the center comes out damp but clean.

Remove the terrine from the water bath and cool completely in the loaf pan on a rack. Cover and chill for at least 4 hours or overnight. To unmold, run a knife around the edges of the terrine and invert carefully onto a serving platter or cutting board.

MAKES ONE 9×5×3-INCH TERRINE (24 SERVINGS)
Per serving: 31 calories (16% from fat), fat: 0.5g, carbohydrates: 3.3g, protein: 3.27g

Herbed Turkey Pâté

*W*ith sliced tomato and crunchy romaine lettuce, this pâté makes a great sandwich.

Turkey breast is the leanest of all meats with only 1 percent fat by weight. Make sure you purchase ground turkey breast (ground turkey containing skin can have as much as 15 percent fat).

Herbes de Provence is an aromatic blend of lavender, fennel, rosemary, and marjoram. It is available in specialty stores and many supermarkets.

1 medium onion, finely chopped
1 celery rib, finely chopped
1 cup finely chopped cauliflower florets
2 1/2 teaspoons dried herbes de Provence
Salt and black pepper
1 pound ground turkey breast

1 tart apple, such as Granny Smith, peeled, cored, and cut into chunks
1/2 cup nonfat cream cheese
1/2 cup Nonfat Yogurt Cheese (page 40)
1/4 teaspoon grated nutmeg
1/2 teaspoon dry mustard

Lightly coat a large skillet with nonstick cooking spray. Add the onion, celery, and cauliflower and sauté over medium heat, stirring often, until the vegetables are tender, 6 to 8 minutes. Stir in the herbes de Provence, a generous pinch of salt, and a few grinds of pepper and cook 2 minutes longer. Transfer to a bowl and set aside. Wipe the pan clean and lightly coat with the nonstick spray once more. Add the ground turkey and sauté, breaking up the meat with a fork, until opaque and no traces of pink are visible, 3 to 4 minutes. Do not brown. Since the meat is so lean, it will become dry and rubbery if overcooked.

Place the cooked turkey in the bowl of a food processor. Add the apple chunks and pulse until finely chopped. Transfer to the bowl containing the celery mixture and let cool completely.

Add the cream cheese, yogurt cheese, nutmeg, and dry mustard to the turkey and blend well to combine. Season to taste with salt and pepper.

Line a 9×5×3-inch loaf pan with plastic wrap. Scrape the turkey mixture into the pan, pressing down firmly to make sure there are no air pockets. Cover and chill for at least 4 hours and up to 24 hours.

MAKES ONE 9×5×3-INCH LOAF (24 SERVINGS)
Per serving: 40 calories (7% from fat), fat: 0.28g, carbohydrates: 2.85g, protein: 6.25g

Three-Bean and Pesto Terrine

This is a very simple and satisfying terrine. It keeps well and can be made several days ahead. Try serving it with wedges of corn bread, sticks of jicama, and slices of the Mexican squash, chayote.

1 (15-ounce) can red kidney
   beans, drained and rinsed
3/4 cup low-fat buttermilk
3/4 teaspoon ground cumin
1 tablespoon tomato paste
Dash of paprika
Salt and black pepper

1 (15-ounce) can cannellini
   beans, drained and rinsed
1 (15-ounce) can pink kidney
   beans, drained and rinsed
Dash of cayenne
1 cup Basil Pesto Spread
   (page 15)

Line a 5-cup terrine pan or mold with plastic wrap.

In the bowl of a food processor, combine the red kidney beans with ¼ cup of the buttermilk, ¼ teaspoon of the cumin, the tomato paste, paprika, and salt and pepper to taste. Process until smooth. Transfer the contents to a small bowl and set aside.

Wipe the food processor clean and add the cannellini beans, ¼ cup of the buttermilk, ¼ teaspoon of the cumin, and salt and pepper to taste. Process until smooth. Transfer to another small bowl and set aside.

Wipe the processor clean again and add the pink beans, the remaining ¼ cup buttermilk, the remaining ¼ teaspoon cumin, the cayenne, and salt and pepper to taste. Process until smooth. Transfer to a third small bowl and set aside.

Spread the red kidney bean mixture in the bottom of the prepared pan, smoothing the top even with a knife. Spread ½ cup of the pesto over the bean layer. This is a little tricky because the pesto has a stiffer texture than the beans. Break it up into little pieces and pat them in place with your fingers until you have an even layer. Next, spread the cannellini bean mixture over the pesto, smoothing with a knife. Repeat another layer of pesto, using the remaining $1/2$ cup. Finish with a layer of the pink bean mixture. Smooth the top of the terrine with a knife, cover with plastic wrap, and chill at least 2 hours before unmolding. The terrine can be made up to 2 days ahead.

To unmold, invert the terrine on a cutting board or serving platter. Rap the bottom a couple of times. Loosen the plastic wrap and gently ease off the mold. Smooth the sides with a knife and serve.

MAKES ONE 5-CUP TERRINE (40 SERVINGS)
Per serving: 33 calories (9% from fat), fat: 0.34g, carbohydrates: 5.94g, protein: 1.96g

Smoked Trout Pâté

*T*his elegant pâté not only looks lovely but tastes out of this world! It would be equally suited to a cocktail party, served on cucumber rounds, or a brunch buffet, served with fresh bagels.

1 cup Nonfat Yogurt Cheese
  (page 40)
1/2 cup flaked smoked trout
  fillet
2 teaspoons prepared
  horseradish
1 tablespoon chopped fresh
  parsley

2 teaspoons lemon juice
1/4 teaspoon salt
Freshly ground black pepper
3 to 4 very thin lemon slices
  (optional)

In a food processor, combine the yogurt cheese, smoked trout, horseradish, parsley, lemon juice, salt, and black pepper and pulse until just combined. Line an 8-ounce mold or ramekin with plastic wrap. Place the lemon slices, if using, in the bottom, overlapping slightly so that they make a spiral covering the bottom of the mold. Scoop the pâté into the mold, using a rubber spatula to compress it, making sure the mold is filled completely. Cover and refrigerate for several hours.

To unmold, uncover the pâté and carefully invert onto a plate. Gently loosen the plastic from the mold and lift the mold straight up. Peel off the plastic and smooth the sides, if necessary, with a small knife dipped in hot water.

MAKES 1 CUP (8 SERVINGS)
Per serving: 65 calories (11% from fat), fat: 0.76g, carbohydrates: 5.7g, protein: 8.52g

Brunch and
Dessert Dips
and Spreads

Honey-Vanilla Yogurt Spread

The smooth, custardlike texture of this spread is sort of a cross between Devon clotted cream and pudding, without all the fat. It tastes absolutely decadent spread on muffins or brown bread, or used as a dip for fresh fruit.

Vanilla extract can be substituted for the vanilla bean. Just heat the honey as directed and remove from the heat. Stir in the vanilla extract and allow to cool.

1 quart nonfat vanilla yogurt	1 vanilla bean, split
²/₃ cup honey	lengthwise

Place the yogurt in a fine-mesh strainer lined with cheesecloth positioned over a bowl. Cover and refrigerate for 12 to 24 hours. Discard the liquid. You should have about $1^1/_2$ cups of thick yogurt remaining.

In a small saucepan, combine the honey and the vanilla bean. Bring to a boil over low heat, stirring constantly. Boil for 1 minute while stirring rapidly. Remove from the heat and allow to cool to room temperature.

Remove the vanilla bean, scraping the insides of the pod to extract the vanilla flecks. This is a bit sticky! Blend the honey with the yogurt. Serve right away at room temperature or chill. The spread will keep for up to 10 days tightly covered in the refrigerator.

MAKES 2 CUPS (16 SERVINGS)
Per serving: 95 calories (1% from fat), fat: 0.09g, carbohydrates: 21.5g, protein: 2.94g

Tropical Fruit Ratatouille

The fruit in this ratatouille can be varied, depending on what is available. Other tropical fruits that could be used include star fruit, passion fruit, guava, and cherimoya. More common fruits such as oranges, grapefruits, plums, and peaches can also be included.

This is delicious served over slices of angel food cake, low-fat frozen yogurt, or sorbet. For an unusual brunch dip, try cutting waffles into bite-sized wedges and using them to scoop up the fruit.

*1 large banana, diced
 $^1/_4$ inch*

*1 medium mango, peeled,
 seeded, and diced $^1/_4$ inch*

*1 medium papaya, peeled,
 seeded, and diced $^1/_4$ inch*

*1 cup $^1/_4$-inch diced pine-
 apple, fresh or canned
 and drained*

*2 kiwifruits, peeled and diced
 $^1/_4$ inch*

Zest and juice of 1 lime

*1 tablespoon frozen orange
 juice concentrate, defrosted*

2 tablespoons sugar

*$^1/_4$ cup shredded unsweetened
 coconut*

Toss the banana, mango, papaya, pineapple, and kiwifruit together in a bowl. In a measuring cup, whisk together the lime zest and juice, orange juice concentrate, and sugar. Pour over the fruit and toss gently to combine. Cover and chill. This is best served within a few hours of preparing. Sprinkle with the coconut just before serving.

MAKES 3 $^1/_2$ CUPS (28 SERVINGS)
Per serving: 26 calories (11% from fat), fat: 0.3g, carbohydrates: 6.1g, protein: 0.26g

Pumpkin Pie Spread

This does taste just like pumpkin pie! Spread it on bagels or toast, or try it as a filling for stuffed French toast.

1¼ cups cooked pureed fresh
or canned pumpkin
⅓ cup low-fat cream cheese,
softened
4 tablespoons light brown
sugar

⅛ teaspoon grated nutmeg
½ teaspoon ground
cinnamon
¼ teaspoon ground allspice
¼ teaspoon ground ginger

Place the pumpkin and cream cheese in a small bowl and blend until smooth. Stir in the brown sugar, nutmeg, cinnamon, allspice, and ginger. Cover and chill for at least 1 hour. This spread will keep for up to 1 week tightly covered in the refrigerator.

MAKES 1½ CUPS (12 SERVINGS)
Per serving: 36 calories (30% from fat), fat: 1.26g, carbohydrates: 5.65g, protein: 1g

Extra-Special Cranberry-Orange Relish

The addition of rose water to this traditional relish is what makes it extra-special. Rose water can be purchased in specialty stores. Serve this relish with turkey or spread on slices of brown bread or corn bread with a little yogurt cheese (page 40).

3 cups cranberries, defrosted
if frozen
1 orange

1 cup sugar
½ teaspoon rose water

If you are using frozen cranberries, pat them between 2 layers of paper toweling to remove excess moisture. Remove the zest from the orange with a paring knife, and discard any white pith. Cut the flesh into chunks and remove all seeds. Place the cranberries, orange zest and pulp, and sugar in a food processor and pulse until coarsely chopped. Do not overprocess or it will become a puree. Transfer to a bowl and stir in the rose water. Cover and chill for at least 24 hours. This relish will keep refrigerated for up to 2 weeks.

MAKES 2¹/₂ CUPS (20 SERVINGS)

Per serving: 50 calories (1% from fat), fat: 0.04g, carbohydrates: 13g, protein: 0.15g

Mango-Lime Puree

I love the tangy sweet-tart taste of this silky puree. It's a great dip for fresh slices of honeydew melon, stem strawberries, or bite-sized cubes of angel food cake. It's also wonderful served over low-fat vanilla ice cream or yogurt, or with fresh sliced bananas.

Zest and juice of 2 limes	*¹/₂ cup water*
¹/₄ cup sugar	*2 large ripe mangoes*

Place the lime zest, lime juice, sugar, and water in a small saucepan. Bring to a boil, lower the heat to medium-low, and simmer until reduced to ¹/₄ cup, about 6 minutes. Set aside to cool slightly.

Peel and seed the mangoes. Place the flesh in food processor and puree. With the motor running, add the lime syrup and process until smooth. Transfer to a bowl, cover, and chill at least 1 hour. The puree will keep tightly covered and refrigerated for several days.

MAKES 2 CUPS (16 SERVINGS)

Per serving: 31 calories (2% from fat), fat: 0.08g, carbohydrates: 8.4g, protein: 0.19g

Burgundy-Pear Butter

A spin-off of the classic dessert pears poached in red wine, this spread is luscious on Irish scones, muffins, or toasted homemade bread. Dried pears and creamed honey are available in specialty and health food stores as well as in some supermarkets.

¹/₂ pound dried pears	*1 (2-inch) piece cinnamon stick*
1¹/₂ cups Burgundy or other	*1 clove*
full-bodied red wine	*¹/₄ cup creamed honey*

Combine the pears, wine, cinnamon stick, and clove in a medium nonreactive saucepan. Bring to a boil over medium-high heat. Reduce the heat and simmer for 5 minutes. Remove from the heat and let stand at room temperature for 45 minutes, until cooled and the pears are very soft.

Using a slotted spoon, remove the pears from the wine and place them in a food processor. Process until they form a smooth, thick paste. Discard the cinnamon stick and clove. Bring the wine to a boil again and continue boiling until it is reduced to about 3 tablespoons. It will be very thick and syrupy. With the food-processor motor running, pour the wine syrup into the pears until incorporated. Transfer to a bowl and stir in the creamed honey. Cover and chill. This spread will keep tightly covered in the refrigerator for up to 2 weeks.

MAKES 1 ¹/₂ CUPS (12 SERVINGS)
Per serving: 92 calories (1% from fat), fat: 0.1g, carbohydrates: 19.6g, protein: 0.44g

Dippers and Spreadees

Curly Baked Tortillas

*W*ho says tortilla chips have to be triangles? These baked curls are much more fun!

    12 (10-inch) corn tortillas   *Salt and pepper*

Preheat the oven to 350°F.

Using a pair of kitchen scissors, cut the tortillas, 2 at a time, in long, wavy strips. Do not worry about making them uniform. Cut S shapes, hooks, spirals—whatever you like!

Lightly spray a baking sheet with nonstick cooking spray. Place the tortillas on the sheet, coat lightly with more spray, sprinkle with salt and pepper, and toss gently. Spread them evenly on the sheet and place in the oven. Bake for 10 to 15 minutes, tossing every 5 minutes. They are done when they are lightly browned, crisp, and curly. Serve warm or cool to room temperature and store in an airtight container.

MAKES ABOUT 24 SERVINGS
Per serving: 33 calories (10% from fat), fat: 0.37g, carbohydrates: 6.99g, protein: 0.85g

Variations. For some different tastes, try sprinkling the chips with about ¼ teaspoon of one of the following seasonings instead of, or along with, the salt and pepper: cumin and oregano · garlic powder · curry powder · paprika and lemon pepper.

SERVING SUGGESTIONS
Green Pea Guacamole (page 18) · Bubbly Baked Pizza Dip (page 58)
Papaya and Cilantro Salsa (page 48) · Roasted Red Pepper Mousse
(page 69) · Chunky Black Bean Dip (page 28)

Crisp Vegetable Chips

These yummy, sweet chips are baked instead of fried. They do not get quite as crisp as fried chips. The key is to slice the vegetables into the very thinnest slices possible. A tool called a mandoline does this the best, but a very sharp knife and a steady hand will also do the trick.

1 very thick, large carrot   *Salt*
1 large sweet potato

Preheat the oven to 325°F.

Peel the carrots and slice on a diagonal into the thinnest possible slices so they are almost transparent. Scrub but do not peel the sweet potatoes and slice crosswise into the thinnest slices possible, again until almost transparent.

Lightly coat 2 sheet pans with nonstick cooking spray. Spread the carrot slices in one layer on one and the sweet potatoes on the other. Sprinkle with salt. Place in the oven and bake for 30 to 35 minutes, turning the slices over and switching the position of the pans halfway through. They are done when slightly shriveled, lightly browned, and crisp; watch carefully so they don't burn. Remove from the oven and cool on a paper towel–lined plate.

MAKES ABOUT 4 CUPS (16 SERVINGS)
Per serving: 23 calories (2% from fat), fat: 0.05g, carbohydrates: 5.33g, protein: 0.47g

SERVING SUGGESTIONS
Spinach and Feta Cheese Dip (page 23) • Moroccan White Bean Dip (page 34) • Velvety Roasted Garlic and Romano Dip (page 38) Asian Butternut Squash Puree (page 19)

Sirloin or Chicken Satay

Sirloin tip steak is very lean and lends itself perfectly to quick grilling. To make slicing the steak thinly easier, try freezing it for 20 minutes, until it begins to firm but is not frozen solid. Be sure to soak the bamboo skewers so they do not burn on the grill.

3 tablespoons soy sauce
1 tablespoon dry vermouth
  or sherry
1 shallot, minced
4 thin slices of peeled fresh
  ginger, slivered

$^1/_2$ pound sirloin tip steak
  or boneless, skinless
  chicken breast, cut into
  $^1/_4 \times {}^1/_2 \times 4$-inch strips

Whisk together the soy sauce, vermouth, shallots, and ginger in a mixing bowl. Place the beef or chicken in the marinade and toss to coat. Cover and chill for up to 1 hour. Meanwhile, soak about 24 bamboo skewers in warm water for 15 minutes.

Preheat the broiler or grill. Thread one strip of meat on each skewer. Broil or grill the satays for 3 to 5 minutes, turning halfway through, until cooked to the desired doneness for sirloin and until the chicken has no traces of pink.

MAKES ABOUT 24 SKEWERS/SERVINGS
Per serving: Sirloin—17 calories (29% from fat), fat: 0.51g, carbohydrates: 0.44g, protein: 2.34g
Chicken—13 calories (9% from fat), fat: 0.1g, carbohydrates: 0.43g, protein: 2.39g

SERVING SUGGESTIONS
Roasted Red Pepper Catsup (page 20) · Savory Cranberry Chutney
(page 55) · Horseradish-Dijon Dip (page 42) · Summer Garden Herb
Salsa (page 52) · Creamy Apricot Curry Dip (page 38)
Honey-Mustard Pretzel Dip (page 36) · Thai Dipping Sauce (page 16)

Try

Light Wheat Scones

These light, puffy scones are great with all sorts of sweet and savory dips and spreads, and lend themselves easily to variation.

1 cup all-purpose white flour
1 cup whole wheat flour
4 teaspoons baking powder
Pinch of salt

1 cup unsweetened
    applesauce
2 tablespoons honey
4 to 5 tablespoons skim milk

Preheat the oven to 375°F. and lightly coat a baking sheet with non-stick spray. In a bowl, sift together the flours, baking powder, and salt. In a small bowl, combine the applesauce, honey, and 3 tablespoons of the milk. Make a well in the center of the dry ingredients and add the applesauce mixture. Stir until just combined. Add more milk, if necessary, 1 tablespoonful at a time, to hold the dough together.

Turn out onto a lightly floured surface. Pat into a disk about 1 inch thick. Transfer to the baking sheet. Cut into 8 wedges and gently separate by $\frac{1}{2}$ inch. Bake for 15 to 20 minutes, until puffed and light golden. Remove from the pan and serve warm or cool on a rack.

MAKES 8 SCONES/SERVINGS
Per scone: 141 calories (3% from fat), fat: 0.46g, carbohydrates: 31.7g, protein: 4.08g

Variations. Add $\frac{1}{4}$ teaspoon crumbled dried rosemary and 1 to 2 tablespoons grated Parmesan cheese to the dough.

Stir $\frac{1}{4}$ cup currants or chopped dried apricots into the dough.

Stir 1 teaspoon lemon, lime, or orange zest into the dry ingredients.

SERVING SUGGESTIONS
*Burgundy-Pear Butter (page 82) • Honey-Vanilla Yogurt
Spread (page 78) • Pumpkin Pie Spread (page 80)*

Grilled Polenta Wedges

Polenta is one of those warming, wonderful comfort foods that everyone loves. Chilled until it hardens and then fried or grilled, it takes on a neutral yet tasty character that matches with all sorts of dips and spreads. Traditional polenta made from medium ground cornmeal takes a lot of time and attention but has the fullest flavor. Instant polenta is much faster and is a perfectly fine substitute. If you are in a pinch, there is a ready-made polenta available in many supermarkets, which is precooked and refrigerated and needs only to be sliced and grilled.

4 cups boiling water
1/2 teaspoon salt, plus additional salt for serving

1 cup medium ground yellow cornmeal or instant polenta

Bring the water and salt to a boil in a heavy-bottomed saucepan. Add the cornmeal in a slow, steady stream, whisking constantly. Reduce the heat to low and cook at a bare simmer, stirring constantly. This takes about 30 minutes for the cornmeal and 10 to 15 minutes for the instant polenta. The polenta is ready when it is smooth, very thick, and pulls away from the sides of the pan when stirred with a wooden spoon.

Lightly coat a sheet pan with nonstick cooking spray. When the polenta is done, quickly spread it on the sheet pan in an even thickness of 1/2 inch. This must be done right away because it stiffens up as it begins to cool. Cover with plastic wrap and refrigerate for at least 4 hours and up to 2 days.

When the polenta is chilled, cut it into wedges about 1 1/2 inches long. Lightly coat a nonstick skillet or stovetop grill with nonstick cooking spray and heat until hot but not smoking. Add the polenta wedges several at a time and cook over medium-high heat, 3 to 4 minutes on each side, until crisp and golden. Transfer to a plate and keep warm while continuing with the remaining wedges. Season with salt, if desired, and serve immediately.

MAKES ABOUT 24 WEDGES/SERVINGS
Per wedge: 21 calories (4% from fat), fat: 0.09g, carbohydrates: 4.47g, protein: 0.5g

SERVING SUGGESTIONS
Plum Tomato and Mint Salsa (page 49)
Panzanella Dip (page 24) · Basil Pesto Spread (page 15)
Roasted Red Pepper Catsup (page 20)
Velvety Roasted Garlic and Romano Dip (page 38)

Crostini

Crostini is a term describing a wide range of cocktail or hors d'oeuvres toasts. Just about any type of bread can be used to make crostini, depending on your preference and what it is going to be served with. It can be the base for a canape or used as a dipper or spreadee. Crostini can also be any size or shape you desire. This is the place to let your imagination go wild.

SUGGESTED BREADS

*Baguette, sliced 1/4 inch thick • French bread, sliced on
a diagonal 1/2 inch thick • Pumpernickel bread
Rye bread • Marble bread • Firm-textured white sandwich bread
Raisin bread • Multigrain bread*

In addition to slicing baguettes and loaves with a serrated knife, presliced bread can be cut using small cookie cutters. Circles, diamonds, hearts, and stars are all possibilities. For holidays, try using more symbolic shapes suited to the season.

When you have selected your bread and shape, preheat the oven to 375°F. Lay the bread pieces in a single layer on a baking sheet and lightly coat them with olive oil spray. Place in the oven for 3 to 5 minutes, watching so they do not burn. When lightly toasted, turn the toasts over, coat with olive oil spray again, and bake for 3 to 5 minutes more. The length of time will vary depending on the type and thickness of the bread.

The crostini can be served as is or rubbed with a half clove of garlic and sprinkled with salt and black pepper for a bit more flavor. Serve warm or at room temperature. The crostini will keep 1 to 2 days in an airtight container at room temperature. If they lose their crispness, pop them in a 350°F. oven for 1 to 2 minutes.

SERVING SUGGESTIONS

Baguette crostini with: Sun-Dried Tomato Spread (page 26)
Basil Pesto Spread (page 15) · Anchoiade (page 44)

Rye crostini with: Salmon Mousse (page 68) · Smoked Trout Pâté
(page 76) · Lentil and Rosemary Pâté (page 67)

Pumpernickel crostini with: Crunchy Creamy Water Chestnut-
Scallion Dip (page 42) · Provençal Saffron-Scented Dip (page 30)
Vidalia Onion and Apple Chutney (page 54)
Extra-Special Cranberry-Orange Relish (page 80)

Raisin bread crostini with: Curried Apricot Chutney (page 50)
Honey-Vanilla Yogurt Spread (page 78)
Burgundy-Pear Butter (page 82)

Blanched and Grilled Vegetables

Many vegetables need only to be washed and sliced to be eligible for the crudité basket. Others are much more palatable when lightly cooked. I like to blanch some vegetables in boiling salted water for several minutes and then rinse them in very cold running water. This helps them retain their natural, bright colors better than steaming. Vegetables can be blanched a day ahead and chilled until serving time, lightening the burden of last-minute preparations.

Following is a timetable for blanching a variety of veggies. Start with enough rapidly boiling salted water to cover the vegetables by 3 inches. The pot should be large enough so that they are not crowded. The times given cook the veggies al dente, which means "to the tooth." Crisp-tender is the ideal doneness for a future dipper.

Asparagus spears · 3 to 4 minutes
Baby carrots · 3 to 4 minutes
Baby squash or zucchini · 3 to 4 minutes
Broccoli florets · 4 to 5 minutes
Brussels sprouts · 6 to 7 minutes
Cauliflower florets · 8 to 9 minutes
Red-skinned new potatoes · 10 to 12 minutes

Grilling vegetables is also a yummy way to serve crudités. Give the veggies a light spray of nonstick spray and sprinkle with salt and pepper. Grill at medium heat and be sure to move the vegetables around so they cook evenly.

Eggplant slices · 5 to 6 minutes
Fennel slices · 5 to 6 minutes
Mushrooms · 1 to 3 minutes
Onion wedges · 6 to 8 minutes
Zucchini and squash slices · 3 to 5 minutes